Praise for *The Shroud: Face to Face*

"This is a compelling and convincing account of the single most fascinating relic in the Christian world. Anyone seeking to understand the significance and history of the Shroud of Turin should read this book."

— Most Reverend Robert Barron, Bishop of Winona-Rochester, Founder of the Global Media Ministry Word on Fire

"Robert Orlando brings his varied background, credentials, and interests to the writing of this volume. His filmmaking pursuits (as in his newest release on the Shroud of Turin) and his personal studies of theology and world religions, while pursuing graduate studies at Princeton Theological Seminary, are some of these features that coalesce in the task of writing this text. Approaching the archaeological artifact that has been studied more than any other in history, Orlando, in producing this fascinating work, combines forensic science, Scripture, and historical studies, all pointing to a possible resurrection event."

— Gary R. Habermas, Ph.D., Distinguished Research Professor, Liberty Baptist Theological Seminary

"Whatever you think about the Shroud's authenticity, Robert Orlando is a skilled filmmaker and a great storyteller, whether in print or on film. His story about this famous relic is bound to tease your heart and mind and ask the question: Could the Shroud provide scientific evidence about the death and Resurrection of Jesus? Well, read the book, see the film with an open mind, and be surprised by where the evidence leads!"

— Ben Witherington, III, Amos Professor of New Testament for Doctoral Studies, Asbury Theological Seminary, emeritus faculty St. Andrews University, Scotland

"Robert Orlando is an impressive filmmaker, writer, and thinker and, to me, a partner. He and I worked together on a book and a film on *The Divine Plan* — the inspiring idea that each of us has a special place and role in this world by Divine Providence. This latest project by Orlando, on the Shroud of Turin, strikes me as his latest contribution to that Divine Plan. Ultimately, that plan brought him face-to-face with the divine mystery of the face of Jesus. His engrossing journey will bring you, too, face-to-face with the Shroud of Turin."

— Paul Kengor, Ph.D., editor of the *American Spectator*, professor of political science at Grove City College, and author of many books, including *The Divine Plan* (co-authored by Robert Orlando)

"I am not a believer in the Shroud, but the subject undeniably remains fascinating, and Orlando's work is both informed and entertaining. Readers will, with his personable guidance, enjoy debating with themselves what they should make of this most famous of all Christian relics."

— Dale C. Allison Jr., Princeton Theological Seminary

"The Shroud of Turin is the most mysterious and controversial Christian artifact that has survived. Could it be the burial shroud of Jesus? Or a medieval forgery, as some think? If so, why can't modern science expose it? Robert Orlando's book adds to the debate and sheds new light on this intriguing mystery."

— Craig A. Evans, John Bisagno Distinguished Professor of Christian Origins, Houston Christian University

The Shroud

Robert Orlando

The Shroud
Face to Face

SOPHIA INSTITUTE PRESS
Manchester, New Hampshire

Cover design by Jason Pearson of Nexus Media.

Sophia Institute Press
Box 5284, Manchester, NH 03108
1-800-888-9344
www.SophiaInstitute.com

paperback ISBN 979-8-88911-028-6

ebook ISBN 979-8-88911-029-3

Library of Congress Control Number: 2023932924

Second printing

I dedicate this book to all who
confront science and historical evidence,
so their faith will never become superstition.

Contents

Foreword

Robert Orlando and I met in Houston at the National Museum of Funeral History — yep, that's a thing, and it's incredible. I had flown in from Rome to lecture on the Shroud of Turin. The writer-director had flown in from Princeton to interview me.

As I sat between bright lights and a green screen, a makeup artist started powdering my face. Not a typical day for this priest-professor. When the interview began, I had no idea who Robert Orlando was or what he was after.

As I was exhausted from hours of lecturing, I scarcely believe that anything coherent came out of my mouth. But apparently my high-energy interlocutor pried from me something of worth. Elated, he called for a cut.

Stepping out of the spotlight, I sighed with relief. Though my body craved sleep, Robert's enthusiasm was infectious. We can rest in heaven, right? So I decided to grab a beer with my new friend.

Amid the playful banter in some Texas steakhouse, we also engaged in a lively philosophical and theological debate. Paul the Apostle and Paul McCartney, Kant and Kierkegaard, Luther and

Ratzinger —their names peppered our conversation. It was a spicy one but intensely fun.

Robert Orlando is a connoisseur of culture who is at his best in this book. It is a sober yet stirring account of his encounter with the figure of Jesus Christ, as it came about while wrestling with this Winding Sheet and grappling with all the data around it — biblical, historical, and scientific.

What is it? Where did it come from? Who is the man depicted here? How was his image formed? What does it all mean?

I love that Orlando allows us to weigh all the evidence and come to our own conclusions. Having been ignorant of Shroud studies for most of my life and even throughout ten years of seminarian formation, I wholeheartedly endorse this approach.

I was shaken out of my ignorance in 2011, when Emanuela Marinelli invited me to a conference on the Shroud of Turin at the Pontifical Athenaeum Regina Apostolorum. Here in Italy, she has played a pivotal role in disseminating knowledge of the Shroud. Orlando's work could serve a similar function in the English-speaking world.

Yes, there are plenty of other voices already out there: Barrie Schwortz, Bruno Barberis, Paolo Di Lazzaro, Gian Maria Zaccone, Pierluigi Baima Bollone, Marco Riani, William Meacham, Joe Marino, Tristan Casabianca, Kelly Kearse, Robert Rucker, Cheryl White — to name just a few researchers who have mentored me.

Still, Orlando is particularly and providentially prepared to tell his unique story, not only because of his penchant for biblical and historical study or even his exceptional skill at filmmaking but, above all, because he has shared in the cross of Christ.

Ultimately, it is a story about an earthshaking, life-altering, face-to-face encounter with the Man called the King of the Jews. *Ecce homo. Ecce rex.* Ever since Adam and Eve (and Cain after them) were exiled "east of Eden," away from the "face [presence] of the Lord," the human heart has ached to regain paradise lost (see Genesis 3:24;

4:16). As St. Augustine put it: "You made us for Yourself, O Lord, and our hearts are restless until they rest in You."

The Scriptures speak of the face-to-face vision of God as our deepest desire, upward calling, and heavenly home. The psalmist sings of it: "Lord, show us the light of your face" (Psalm 4:6, NAB). Such eschatological hunger compelled the cry of the Greeks to Philip, "Sir, we wish to see Jesus" (John 12:21). It stirred a vertically challenged tax collector named Zacchaeus to climb a sycamore (Luke 19:4). It was the reason Peter wished to remain on the Mount of the Transfiguration (see Matthew 17:4).

But the fullness of heaven lies beyond our earthly horizon. Sure, angels look on God's face (Matthew 18:10). But we long to "see him as he is" (1 John 3:2). *As he is* — to my mind, these words translate well the meaning of *face-to-face* encounter. Indeed, Christians understand the Beatific Vision to be the direct and intuitive vision of God's essence, without the mediation of any creature.

"For now we see in a mirror dimly" (1 Corinthians 13:12). As it happens, the face impressed upon the Turin Shroud is dim and mirrored. It is brutally disfigured, and the eyes are closed. And yet the expression of this dead man is profoundly peaceful.

In light of our present station on Earth and our future home in heaven, the image on the Shroud could hardly be more fitting. For me, it captures two central mysteries of the Christian profession: the incarnation and the resurrection.

By his in-flesh-ment, God immortal assumed our mortal nature to accomplish in it a saving sacrifice. This descent into death climaxed paradoxically on a Friday Christians call "Good." On Resurrection Sunday, he rose to glory, thereby vindicating his claim of being the dying and rising Davidic Messiah and Son of God.

The Shroud bears witness to the twofold dimension of the Paschal Mystery: "Dying, you destroyed our death. Rising, you restored our life."

Just as Jesus' death should not be separated from his resurrection, so the cross should not be separated from the Shroud. As often noted, the former received him alive and handed him over dead, but the latter received him dead and handed him over alive again.

In my view, the enigmatic image of the Shroud that exists ultimately finds its best explanation in the resurrection of that dead body. It is the natural effect of a supernatural event.

Of course, you mustn't take my word for it. Come with your skepticism, if you must. After all, Jesus did not stiff-arm Doubting Thomas. He invited him to probe his wounds. Today, the Savior humbly exposes himself to scrutiny by means of the Shroud.

"Put your finger here, and see my hands; and put out your hand, and place it in my side; do not be faithless, but believing." In light of what he saw, Thomas replied, "My Lord and my God!" (John 20:27–28). And so Christ's question remains for each of us: "But who do you say that I am?"

This beautiful book offers us a fresh opportunity to respond.

— Fr. Andrew Dalton, L.C., S.T.D.
Professor of Theology,
Pontifical Athenaeum Regina, Apostolorum

The Shroud

Introduction

My fascination with the Shroud and its meaning in the Western world is relatively new, though as an author, a filmmaker, and a person immersed in biblical studies, I have long explored the ancient world, the apostles, and the origins of the Church.

Two weeks before the Christmas of 2021, on a snowy eve in New York City, I was to appear in a TV interview on my previous film, *The Divine Plan*. The discussion was followed by a Plaza Hotel party, a who's who of TV personalities. One of the executives asked if I would ever consider a film about the Shroud.

Strangely, the subject was brought to me by one of my film partners, who was working on establishing a Shroud center in California. My answer to the network and my partner was "fascinating, but not for me." I had too much on my plate. Privately, I was also suspicious of relics and pet theories about the ancient past — or so I thought.

Fast-forward two weeks later to Christmas Eve, 2021. My father was recovering in the hospital from a nasty fall but was improving and set for rehab when he died unexpectedly. The suddenness of his death, the shock of it all, stirred something unfinished in me. It raised questions that didn't, at that moment, have answers.

I needed a sign that my father was okay.

In the weeks after the funeral, as I sorted through his letters to me — which he wrote to encourage my lifelong journey of truth and faith — I turned away from films and books and turned inward, toward writing fiction and poetry. I even decided to pursue my graduate studies at Princeton Theological Seminary with a well-known Jesus scholar, Dale Allison, also versed in the Shroud.

Still, I remembered the weeks before my father died, when my partner, the network executive, asked if I had ever considered the Shroud of Turin as a subject. Was it a coincidence when I was about to dive back into the ancient world of Jesus and his passion and resurrection?

The Shroud was one of many relics I had encountered over the years. As a Catholic, I had been to Europe and was familiar with many relics and icons of faith. I watched History Channel and BBC documentaries on the subject. I realized that they featured experts clashing on the historical and scientific facts — a challenge similar to my work in biographies, books, and films.

Another factor that compelled me was that, although I had written about early Christianity, I had never explored the biography of Jesus. I knew the Gospels well, but was I ready to retake this journey with the Shroud as a critical piece of evidence to reopen my investigation: a new crime scene to unearth the nature of the Shroud?

My odyssey began, and the route became clearer. Not only would my journey connect a new piece of science with the ancient biblical past; I envisioned it as the Greatest Scientific Project Ever Told. It intrigued the scholar and the detective in me. What if this was the Shroud that enveloped Jesus? What if it matched early Scripture to make a science-based story, or even a kind of fifth Gospel — a living witness to Jesus Christ?

I needed to set up a grid and uncover the crime scene: Golgotha, "the place of a skull,"[1] where I could find the cross and the body no longer in the tomb. Jesus' followers say that he was raised from the dead. Of course, the skeptics don't buy it. Could they be right? Were the early Christians simply delusional with grief? Were they hallucinating? Or was it some grand conspiracy to trick others into worshipping their dead leader?

No. I knew there was more here to the man in the Shroud than a charlatan.

My discovery would uncover not an ancient myth but, with the help of the Shroud, a potential forensic pathway into something extraordinary, if not supernatural.

I realized my journey began when I was a young teenager who prayed: "God, if you're there, make yourself real to me." Could the recent loss of my father be another question, leading me to challenge a new generation hidden behind clouds of skepticism?

The way forward would be to trace the biblical roots, travel to ancient sites, interview experts, and explore the latest technology. Science keeps evolving, and new clues are bound to come to light.

Other than written testimony, and the experiences of believers, we had little scientific evidence of Jesus' life until the discovery of the Shroud.

As a person who has studied Christianity, I know that the church teaches that not only can our personal or spiritual experiences lead us to truth, but so can the study of nature and the sciences. By studying the Shroud through the lens of science, we can learn more about the man Jesus.

Paul writes in his Letter to the Romans that God shows himself in the natural things of the world, including those as simple as a flower, or childbirth, or a sunset, and that all these creations point to an unfathomable and infinite source of light, goodness, and beauty.[2] Paul clearly believes that all people, through their innate ability to reason, can know God through the study of his creation.

The question is, how do we approach a story that makes metaphysical claims in a world concerned with only material phenomena? Well, we let the facts and testimonies and the science speak for themselves.

I envisioned that the story would look like any crime scene viewed through a scientific lens. I would follow the facts. What if, along with the Bible and the church's teachings, God was revealing himself through science — something that would revolutionize the faith? A simple story about a man who influenced a two-thousand-year history?

As I redraw the chalk lines, would I find that the image on the Shroud was that of Jesus and finally reconcile faith and science, forcing the present world to come face-to-face with the figure of Christ?

Let's open the case.

I'll begin with the story of the Shroud of Turin through two millennia in which theories, beliefs, and scientific discoveries often collided. As I did with many of my projects, especially the books and films on the apostle Paul, I will sort through Greek texts with their firsthand accounts.

Many believers have found in the Shroud support for belief in the life of Jesus Christ. Some believe the relic is a forgery or a mysterious phenomenon. For others, the Shroud is evidence of Jesus' resurrection. If the latter are right, then this single piece of forensics both works with and transcends the laws of chemistry and physics.

Many scientific, archaeological, and historical experts conclude that the linen held a body that was beaten and had absorbed significant radiation before being transformed. But what lies behind these confident, dramatic, and far-reaching assertions?

This book is part of the effort to answer that question and others. It hopes to win over skeptics — not only atheists, but fellow Christians too. Doubts about the Shroud's authenticity are rife. For instance, well-known Protestant scholar John Calvin asked, "How is it possible that those sacred historians, who carefully related all the miracles that took place at Christ's death, should have omitted to mention one so remarkable as the likeness of the body of our Lord remaining on its wrapping sheet?"

I want to take those doubts seriously. I am not one to select a biased group of scientists to prove that another group is wrong. I intend to provide a full report: the crime scene, the blood results, the testimonies, and the forensic evidence to construct a true narrative before testing the story against Holy Writ.

First, we must find a plausible scientific answer, even if it pointed to a mysterious ending. I had a team of experts, and a daunting amount of literature remained on the subject. Whether it be books, documentaries, or the Internet, a plethora of modern sources miss the connection between faith and science. So how is an author, filmmaker, and historian of early Christianity to evaluate such phenomena?

Dale Allison reminds us, "Most of us know nothing — absolutely nothing — about Maillard reactions, colorimetric measurements, low-energy radiography, thermal neutron flux, or pyrolysis mass spectrometry."[3]

But the truths that the Shroud points to really can be grasped by anyone. All we need to do is establish a timeline, a list of possible suspects, and witnesses and draft a plausible narrative that explains the collective facts. Who was there, and what was the crime for which Jesus was accused? How was he crucified, and how was he placed in his tomb?

The skeptic and the cynic must also ask, "If the Gospel accounts are wrong, how else can we explain Jesus' missing body — and the Shroud he left behind?"

We can't dismiss offhand the unknown or metaphysical possibilities beyond our present scientific knowledge. The fact is that whatever occurred at that moment in time had to have happened inside the tomb. Our crime scene must be explained from the inside out and involve a source of light, the witness of others, and the only evidence left.

According to Jesus' followers, who lived in fear of their own martyrdom, the authorities watched the body of Jesus and testified that it was missing, or at least that it was not stolen. According to Jesus' apostles, God raised him from the dead. Can the ultimate answers be found in the Shroud?

Was it meant to confront the skeptic with the most significant challenge: how one might rethink religious phenomena in scientific terms and reflect once again on Jesus face-to-face — hearing his voice asking, "Who do you say I am?"

Prologue

According to ancient tradition, a star was formed in anticipation of his birth. The King of Judea feared him, wanted him dead. There were rumors that one day the Holy One would rise as King. Had he been found, he would have been murdered.

He was baptized by a prophet. He spent forty days alone in the desert, contemplating his Father's will and being tempted by the evil one.

At thirty years old, he would publicly preach controversial religious ideas to the masses. Legend was that he would heal the lame, cure the sick, and restore sight to the blind. He went on to gather a massive following and challenged the religious authorities.

He would then be taken from his brethren, accused of a crime, and tortured. But he had committed no apparent crime. Was he set up, framed? After days of beatings, he was crucified at the place of the skull.

Dark clouds would blot out the light as he convulsed and bled on the cross.

And for the high holy days, he would lie in a dark tomb, wrapped in linen, peaceful but soon to be forgotten — or so the authorities hoped. When his friends came, they were amazed to find nothing but his burial cloths and an empty tomb.

Where was the body?

His friends proclaimed that he was no longer there but had arisen, which would spark a scandal that has lasted two thousand years.

Skeptics would claim this was all his followers' fantasies that he had risen from the dead and reappeared. But their eyewitness testimony would be supported with a new piece of forensic evidence: his Shroud.

What do the witnesses have to say about this man Jesus, who claimed equality with God? Can the Shroud lead us to the missing body? Or is this a cold case, a murder and a missing body from two thousand years ago that will never be solved?

1

A Holy Crime Scene

Jesus, son of Joseph and Mary, was raised in humble beginnings in what might be considered, in today's terms, "the sticks": Nazareth.[4] He was born in even humbler settings: an animals' stable. As a boy, he was presumably trained by his father, Joseph, in the art of carpentry and worked at his father's craft until he was about thirty years old.

According to the Gospels, the four biblical books (Matthew, Mark, Luke, and John) that narrate Jesus' life, that's when his controversial teaching ministry began.[5] No one expected that Jesus, son of the carpenter Joseph, would die a criminal's death by crucifixion and wind up at the center of one of the largest religions in the history of the world.

There is very little information about Jesus' early life, besides a few biblical vignettes, such as him teaching in the Temple as a twelve-year-old; history is silent on his early life. But when he embarked on his preaching years, people started to pay attention. Many adored him. Many more sought his downfall. Some plotted his murder.

Could political or religious motives alone explain this man's death?

Jesus' teachings reportedly enraged Israel's religious leaders. They felt that his teachings contradicted their laws and undermined their authority. Jesus did openly, and repeatedly, condemn the behavior of certain Jewish authorities.[6]

But it went beyond that. The Gospels also say that Jesus identified himself with God. He claimed to have the power to forgive sins. He seemed to suggest that he would destroy the Jewish Temple and rebuild it in three days.[7] And he vowed that he would rise after dying. Rumor had it that he would then rule the Kingdom of God, as the Anointed One.[8]

To the Pharisees, Jesus' claim to divinity was blasphemy.

And the Romans, too, had good reason to fear Jesus.

As soon as he began preaching, this Nazarene began amassing a larger and larger following. Many believed that this Jesus — not Herod, not Caesar — was the true king of Israel. Rumors even spread that he called himself God. The emperors of Rome were fond of making the same claim for themselves and didn't appreciate it when itinerant preachers on the far-flung fringes of their empire tried to undermine their authority.

Before the annual Passover celebration, Jesus made a grand entrance into Jerusalem.[9] He rode into the city on a donkey, in contrast to Caesar, who would enter the city on a stallion.[10] Surely Jesus was mocking them!

A large crowd met him at the entrance to Jerusalem.[11] People pushed forward to have the honor of welcoming the Messiah — the Anointed One — and paving Jesus' path with palms. *Messiah* meant "king" in the physical sense. The term wasn't symbolic.[12] As far as Jesus' followers were concerned, Jesus was here as the Davidic Messiah to restore the Kingdom of God on Earth. At the time, religion and politics were tightly intertwined; thus, few if any would have believed that Jesus would not overthrow the powers that be.[13]

Jesus had instigated a movement — a movement that neither the Sadducees nor the Pharisees, neither the Romans nor the Herodians, could control.

Jesus and his twelve apostles gathered in the famous Upper Room to have what is now considered his Last Supper. The Synoptic Gospels say that the Last Supper was in celebration of the Jewish Passover.[14] John's Gospel records that this was the evening before the Passover. But all four Gospels similarly portray the Last Supper as a New Passover, instituted by Jesus.

The holiday Passover commemorated the Israelites' escape from Egyptian captivity under the leadership of Moses. Many scholars think the year was somewhere between AD 30 and 33.[15]

According to the Gospels, one of Jesus' twelve closest followers, known as Judas Iscariot, was not convinced of Jesus' claims of divinity.[16] John's Gospel reports that he did not support the extravagance in which Jesus sometimes dined. He was often the guest of those who — like Mary, the sister of Lazarus — would shower him with offerings such as food and oil.

According to the Bible, Judas would turn Jesus over to the Jewish authorities in exchange for thirty pieces of silver.[17]

The evidence suggests that the Last Supper likely took place in a remote residence near the residence of the high priest, Caiaphas, on Mount Zion, south of the city wall. If this were the correct location, Judas and Caiaphas could quickly contact each other and swiftly follow through on their plot to arrest Jesus.

Judas revealed the location of the Last Supper to the Jewish authorities that night. The Synoptic Gospels claim that while Judas and the Jewish authorities were conspiring to arrest Jesus, Jesus was praying in the Garden of Gethsemane with his disciples.[18] John's Gospel places Jesus in the Kidron valley, "where there was a garden."[19]

Reportedly, this is the scene of the arrest. Caiaphas's men were able to efficiently sweep Jesus away to the high priest's residence, where he was questioned by Caiaphas and the Jewish guards.

Jesus was then interrogated by the Sanhedrin. Under interrogation, he claimed that he was the Son of God. Caiaphas accused him of blasphemy and demanded that he be punished by death.[20]

Jesus reportedly also had allies in the crowd. Joseph of Arimathea, a member of the Sanhedrin, and Nicodemus, a Pharisee and member of the Sanhedrin, believed that Jesus was innocent. What they did not yet reveal is that they believed Jesus really was the Messiah. But it was no use. The secret Christians were outnumbered.

Why did the Jewish authorities not stone Jesus then and there? Judea was a Roman province. Nobody had the authority to impose capital punishment except the local governor, Pontius Pilate. Besides, Caiaphas knew that killing the leader of such a popular movement would have led to a riot.

The safest option was to pin Jesus' blood on Rome. So the Jewish authorities brought Jesus to Pilate to petition for execution.[21]

Caiaphas tried to sway the Roman authorities by framing Jesus as a usurper. He proclaimed himself "King of the Jews," Caiaphas said.[22] And if Rome thinks someone is claiming kingship over Caesar, that someone is guilty of sedition — the punishment for which is death.

Pilate questioned Jesus but reportedly did not find any proof that Jesus was guilty of any crime against Roman law.[23] Taking what was likely a calculated political maneuver to avoid confronting the Pharisees and the increasingly rowdy crowd, Pilate offered to release one Jewish prisoner.[24]

The Gospels note that this had become a custom: Pilate offered to release one prisoner every Passover, as a token of goodwill toward the Jewish people.[25]

The crowd was given the choice between Jesus and a zealot named Barabbas. They chose Barabbas. Now Pilate, who, according to the Gospel record, had Jesus beaten, sentenced Jesus to the ultimate death — death by crucifixion — for a crime he didn't commit.

The Roman officers brutally tortured Jesus. The Gospels mention that he was flogged repeatedly and spat on. One of the soldiers made a crown out of thorns and placed it on Jesus' head, mocking his claim to be the King of the Jews.

The wooden cross was being assembled. Pilate drew up the inscription for a placard that was to read "King of the Jews" and to be fixed above Jesus on the cross.

The path that Jesus took to Calvary is disputed. Today, many believe that Christ's march to Calvary follows the traditional Via Dolorosa (Latin for "Way of Suffering"), a half-mile march. Christ reportedly collapsed and paused several times along the way due to severe physical exhaustion.

The Synoptic Gospels report that at one point, another man, Simon of Cyrene, carried the cross as Jesus was no longer able to bear the weight.[26]

Contrary to common perception, Jesus likely did not carry the entire cross to Golgotha. The two wooden beams could have weighed upwards of two hundred pounds, a nearly unbearable burden for even a healthy man, not to mention one who had been whipped and tortured beforehand. It's more likely that Jesus carried the patibulum, the horizontal beam of the cross. Even that would have been quite a burden — perhaps sixty pounds — for a man with lung and muscle damage, with wooden splinters digging into the whip wounds with the bounce of each step on the trek to Calvary.[27]

The Hebrew name for Calvary is Golgotha, which fittingly means, "the place of the skull."[28] The Gospels give very little information on Jesus' path to Golgotha.[29]

There are accounts of places like Golgotha in the historical record:

> According to Tacitus there was a special place in Rome for the punishment of slaves . . . where no doubt numerous crosses were set up. We learn from Annals 2.32.2 that this horrific place was on the Campus Esquilinus, the counterpart of the hill of Golgotha in Jerusalem. As a result, Horace calls the vulture the Esquiline bird . . . and Juvenal describes the grisly way in which it disposes of corpses even in Rome. (Satires 14.77f.): "The vulture hurries from dead cattle and dogs and crosses . . . to bring some of the carrion to her offspring."[30]

Jesus would have grown up in the shadow of the cross. Rome used crucifixion as a fear tactic. Crucifixion was the most gruesome of all punishments. It was the ultimate crime deterrent. It was so horrible that Roman historians and writers refrained from mentioning it in their works.[31]

Sometimes thousands of people were crucified at once. In the Gospel accounts, Jesus was not the only one crucified that day. Beside him hung two criminals, either thieves or terrorists.

In a Roman crucifixion, the condemned person's wrists and feet or ankles would be nailed to the cross. Some experts theorize that asphyxiation was the main cause of death on a cross, on top of other factors, such as dehydration and exposure to the elements.[32] It's likely that the crucified would have to push up on his feet to avoid suffocating.

When the crucified could no longer push himself up, his arms would pull up on his chest, preventing him from exhaling properly and, thus, leading to suffocation. The Romans would add seats like the footrests to prolong the suffering. The crucified would be exposed to the elements. Crows would pick away his flesh. The Romans maximized their suffering.

If they needed to speed up the process, the Roman soldiers would sometimes break the criminal's legs so he could no longer support himself. But they did not do this to Jesus. They didn't have to. He died within three hours of being hung on the cross, which was unusually fast, even for such a horrific form of execution.

We know, therefore, that Jesus was brutally beaten ahead of time.

Not only was he crucified, but all the Gospels give accounts of Jesus' burial. The name of the hill where Jesus was crucified, Golgotha, suggests that skulls might have littered the hill, indicating that some bodies were left behind. Dogs would come and pick at every part but the skulls.

Crucifixion was generally reserved for outlaws, slaves, and dangerous criminals. (Roman citizens were not crucified.) So, oftentimes, the families and friends of those crucified did not have the means for a proper burial.

In the Jewish law, the bodies of the dead had to be put in the ground before sunset, before the Sabbath. It was against Jewish law to cleanse bodies on the Sabbath.[33] Joseph of Arimathea — Jesus' supporter in the Sanhedrin — volunteered to take Jesus' body down, prepare it for burial, and place it in his own tomb. John's Gospel reports that Nicodemus, the Christian Pharisee, was also intimately involved in the burial. Both men asked permission from Pontius Pilate to bury Jesus and were granted their request.[34] Nicodemus brought nearly a hundred Roman pounds of aloes and myrrh with him to the tomb.[35] That wasn't cheap. These were men with high social standing who had the clout to retrieve Christ's body from the Romans and to donate a rock-hewn tomb.

Joseph of Arimathea brought the body to the large, unoccupied tomb,[36] which was not far from the cross. Mary Magdalene and "the other Mary" were reportedly there too.[37] Normally they would have anointed the body, but since it was so close to sundown, they had to wait until after the Sabbath, their observed day of rest.[38]

Matthew reports that the Jewish authorities petitioned Pilate to station guards at the tomb. Some scholars question the historicity of Matthew's claim and argue that the narrative of the guards was pure Christian apologetics, to fend off accusations of body snatching.[39] The theory is that early Christians would have had every motive to defend the historicity of the resurrection, the cornerstone of their beliefs.[40]

Although it is not possible at present to prove or disprove whether guards were stationed outside Jesus' tomb, it would seem highly unlikely that the Jewish authorities would leave the place unguarded. They had every motive to keep it under watch. Their great fear was that the man whom they fought to put to death would live on in the culture and traditions of his followers. They were afraid not only of the man but also of the movement he inspired, which constituted a break from Judaism and therefore the Jewish authorities' grip on Israel. They had a clear motive to protect the tomb.

According to Matthew, the Jewish authorities feared that Jesus' disciples were planning to steal the body in order to prove Jesus' claim that he would rise again:

> Next day, that is, after the day of Preparation, the chief priests and the Pharisees gathered before Pilate and said, "Sir, we remember how that imposter said, while he was still alive, 'After three days I will rise again.' Therefore order the sepulchre to be made secure until the third day, lest his disciples go and steal him away, and tell the people, 'He has risen from the dead,' and the last fraud will be worse than the

first." Pilate said to them, "You have a guard of soldiers; go, make it as secure as you can." So they went and made the sepulchre secure by sealing the stone and setting a guard.[41]

Pilate gave them the guard they requested. If Matthew's story is accurate, there were probably at least two Roman guards, because, according to the Jewish authorities, it took two witnesses to establish a truthful testimony in court.[42] It would make sense that the Jewish authorities would post their own guard as well, to have someone they personally trusted. Recall that they used their own police force to arrest Jesus at Gethsemane.[43]

It wasn't unheard of that a guard or "custodian" would be present at the tombs of executed criminals. The law prohibited the removal and honoring of men whom the state had executed. The custodian would ensure that the criminals would not be mourned.[44]

It seems likely that two powerful authorities had a vested interest in keeping the body in the tomb. The Romans would want to keep the peace, and the Jewish authorities would not want to give the Christians' religious claims more credence.

When the women showed up on Sunday morning, the first daylight opportunity after the Sabbath and the Passover to go to the tomb,[45] the stone had been rolled to the side and the body was gone. The murder of Jesus of Nazareth, son of Joseph the carpenter, took an unexpected twist. As the Gospels reflect, not even Jesus' followers expected this.

Could it be true? Could he have been raised from the dead?

If not, where did the body go?

If this extraordinary legend is true, and Jesus is the Son of God, then the world would be changed forever. The risen King would be deserving not only of great honor but of worship — worship as the one true God.

2

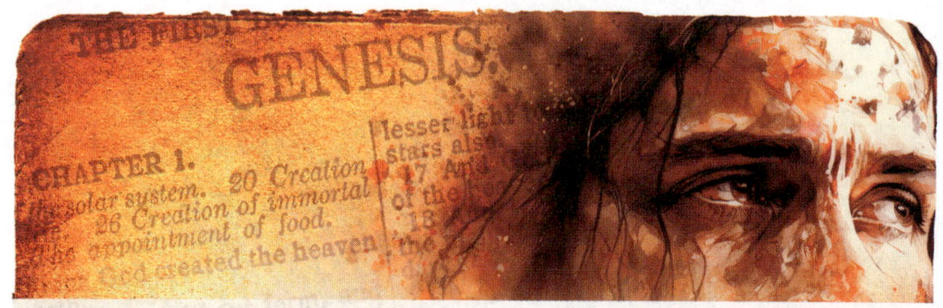
GENESIS.
CHAPTER 1.
20 Creation
solar system.
26 Creation of immortal
appointment of food.
lesser light
stars also.

#8
#12
#6
#3
#10
#7
EXHIBIT 2
EXHIBIT 13

Recorded History

Who was Jesus Christ? Some would say that Jesus was a figment of the Christian imagination, "a savior god who gets historicized."[46] They'd say he was not even a historical figure, casting doubt on one of the most consequential figures in history.

As we will see in our investigation, the Jesus skeptics (or so-called mythicists) are few, and the evidence overwhelmingly points to the reality of the existence of a historical Jesus.[47]

Robert Price is one of the foremost skeptics who denies the existence of a historical Jesus. He used to be Christian, but after conducting research of the origins of the New Testament, he concluded that Jesus is a fiction. He sees parallels between the Christian story of Jesus and ancient religions about gods who die and rise — the pattern of many great myths. He holds that the similarities are too similar to be coincidental.

"I eventually found myself gravitating to that crazy view, that Jesus hadn't existed," he writes, "that he was mythic all the way down, like Hercules. I do not hold it as a dogma. I do not prefer that it be true. It is just that the evidence now seems to me to point that way. The burden of proof would seem to belong with those who believe there was an historical man named Jesus."[48]

Additionally, Price notes that there is a lack of specific references to Jesus in the epistles, or letters, in the New Testament written to specific people or groups. Price claims that the stories of Jesus in the epistles are borrowed from Middle Eastern lore:

> The Jesus story as attested in the Epistles shows strong parallels to Middle Eastern religions based on the myths of dying-and-rising gods. . . . Originally celebrating the seasonal cycle and the yearly death and return of vegetation, these myths were reinterpreted later when peoples of the ancient nationalities relocated around the Roman Empire and in urban settings. The myths now came to symbolize the re-birth of the individual initiate as a personal rite of passage, namely new birth. Strong evidence from ancient stelae and tablets make clear that Baal and Osiris were believed to be dying-and-rising gods long before the Christian era. There is also pre-Christian evidence for the resurrection of Attis, Adonis and Dumuzi/Tammuz. All these survived into the Hellenistic and Roman periods, when they were available to influence Christianity.[49]

Price believes that without physical proof, without having lived in the time of Jesus and having seen firsthand whether he existed, all we have is probabilities. He concedes that it is not outside the realm of possibility that Jesus existed, but "unless someone discovers his diary or his skeleton, we'll never know."[50]

In his book *Deconstructing Jesus,* Price also presents the argument that the Gospels resemble other ancient romance fictions. He says he can identify three "major plot devices" that occur in both the Gospels and other ancient Greek romances in which a man's lover is presumed dead, and through a series of trials and periods of confusion, the man eventually reunites with the woman, who wasn't dead after all.

But, again, Price belongs to a small minority of scholarly voices. Most historians attest to the fact that there was a historical Jesus. They hold that even outside Christian tradition and the Bible (which, as a historical document, should not be overlooked), there is evidence for the existence of Jesus.

At the time of Jesus, most people could not read or write. The literacy rate among the population in ancient times was 10 to 15 percent.[51] Up to 95 percent of the population of rural Galilee could not even read.[52] Learning to read and write was typically the hallmark of an elite education, reserved for those in society with means. So, understandably, there are few surviving written testimonies from this era. Nonetheless, several such testimonies (besides the Gospels) mention a Jesus who was crucified under Pontius Pilate and launched a revolutionary religion.

The pagan Roman historian Tacitus also seems to mention Jesus.[53] According to Martin Hengel's book *Crucifixion in the Ancient World and the Folly of the Message of the Cross,* "Tacitus speaks no less harshly of a 'pernicious superstition' and knows of the shameful fate of the founder: Christus, from whom the name had its origin, suffered the extreme penalty during the reign of Tiberius at the hands of the procurator Pontius Pilate."[54] This matches the historical context outlined in the Gospels, which mention that both Tiberius and Pilate were in office at the time of Jesus' crucifixion.

There's also evidence of a historical Jesus in Flavius Josephus's testimonies.[55] Josephus was a Jewish politician turned historian. He recounts Jesus' ministry and the impact he left on society:

> At this time there appeared Jesus, a wise man, if indeed one should call him a man. For he was a doer of startling deeds, a teacher of people who receive the truth with pleasure. And he gained a following both among many Jews and among many of Greek origin. He was the Messiah. And when Pilate, because of an accusation made by the leading men among us, condemned him to the cross, those who had loved him previously did not cease to do so. For he appeared to them on the third day, living again, just as the divine prophets had spoken of these and countless other wondrous things about him. And up until this very day the tribe of Christians, named after him, has not died out.[56]

Biologist and writer Gerard Verschuuren notes that several other historians living in the time of the budding Christian Church testify to Jesus' existence and the belief of early Christians in Jesus. For example, Suetonius (ca. 69–122), a Roman historian, wrote that a "Chrestus" started a new, controversial religious movement. Pliny the Younger (ca. 62–113), the governor of Bithynia, a Roman province in Asia, wrote about how Christians would pray to Christ. A Greek satirist who lived in the second century, Lucas of Samosata, also wrote about the Christians worshipping Christ.[57]

In light of these sources, it seems not only possible but likely that Jesus existed. The testimonials of these early historians must be considered when evaluating the foundation for the basis of Christianity. To discount these historical sources altogether as evidence for the historical Jesus would mean that the existence of other well-known historical figures with even fewer written testimonies would be thrown into question.[58] We, as a culture, rely on similar testimonies in the historical record for other great historical figures such as Julius Caesar and Alexander the Great.[59]

We also shouldn't overlook the New Testament as a valuable source of historical information.

Of course, not everyone agrees. New Testament scholar and agnostic Bart Ehrman argues that the Bible is unreliable factually: "When I allowed that there could be actual contradictions I started finding them and wow there are a lot more of these that I thought.... The Bible does have mistakes.... The Gospels do have contradictions in them and some of these contradictions cannot plausibly be reconciled and that affects the historical reliability of the accounts."[60]

But contrary to what Price says, the most compelling case of a historical Jesus, which even Ehrman would concede, comes from the record of the Apostle Paul:

> With respect to Jesus, we have numerous, independent accounts of his life in the sources lying behind the Gospels (and the writings of Paul)—sources that originated in Jesus' native tongue Aramaic and that can be dated to within just a year or two of his life (before the religion moved to convert pagans in droves). Historical sources like that are pretty astounding for an ancient figure of any kind.[61]

Some scholars say that up to fourteen letters (although the Pauline authorship of the Letter to the Hebrews is doubted[62]) in the biblical canon were written by the apostle Paul, but it is virtually undisputed that at least seven are Paul's handiwork.[63] These are known as the "consensus letters," and scholars estimate that they were written around AD 50 or 60.

Paul's letters present a no-holds-barred account of the life of Jesus and the beginnings of early Christianity. Paul claims to have known Jesus' family members and leaders of the early Church.[64] He knows James, whom he calls the brother of Jesus, and in fact seems in clear tension with him.[65]

Many scholars (and most Catholics) believe that James was Jesus' cousin. In ancient Israel, the term *brother* was used for any male member of one's extended family.[66] Either way, if anyone were able to testify to Jesus' existence, it would be a family member.[67]

Other books of the New Testament that chronicle the origins of Christianity, such as Luke's Acts of the Apostles, can be viewed as books with great historical value. Ben Witherington III, professor of New Testament for Doctoral Studies at Asbury Theological Seminary, argues that Luke intentionally wrote Acts as a historical report of the developments of the budding Christian movement:

> Luke is not writing either about remote utopian societies, secret religious sects and rites, or words and deeds that he feels are immune to historical scrutiny. His claim is that the Jesus movement and the rise of Christianity are real historical phenomena that at least from time to time touch on the larger historical events and processes of the Empire (hence the synchronisms), and so are subject to careful historical scrutiny in an ancient mode, which is to say, with some openness to claims about the supernatural.[68]

Frankly, there is more evidence to verify the existence of the historical Jesus as the origin of Christianity than there is for Caesar's account of the Gallic Wars. Though scholars might be applauded for denying the former and shunned for denying the latter.

Additionally, we have more than 5,600 manuscripts of the Greek New Testament.[69] Some of the fragments of the papyri date back to the second century AD. So we may say that there is more papyrus and logical evidence for the events that were recorded in the New Testament than any other comparable ancient document. Nobody in classical studies denies the existence of Homer or Alexander the Great, yet their existence is not so well established as Jesus'.

As Ehrman, the Bible critic, states in one of his books:

> Unfortunately, history cannot be written simply on the basis of what makes sense. It makes best sense to me, for example, to think there should never have been influenza epidemics, tsunamis, hurricanes, earthquakes, mudslides, world wars, killing fields, and black deaths that have wiped millions of otherwise innocent and well-meaning people off the face of the earth. But like it or not, disasters happen, whatever my preferences and best sense. History has to be written on the basis of evidence.[70]

And, as the overwhelming majority of historians agree, the evidence shows that Jesus of Nazareth did indeed exist.

Some of the sources give intimate details about his life, what he said, what he did, why eyewitnesses responded to him the way they did, and why there is a Christian church today, two thousand years later.

3

The Witnesses

An empty tomb, a missing body, a bloody shroud. What do the eyewitnesses at the scene of the crime think happened? Did Jesus rise from the dead, as he claimed he would? Is there evidence that the legend is indeed fact?

The body of evidence seems to suggest that Jesus was a real man with a family, friends, and enemies. He was portrayed as being controversial in life but even more so in death.

He was unjustly tried for a crime that not even the Roman authorities believed he committed, but he was still put to death, if only to quell the fears of the power-hungry leaders at the time. The how and why of his death are quite obvious.

The real question is: What happened to him after his death? There is no record of his body being found. The Gospels have no records of anyone claiming to have recovered the body. Initially, not even Jesus' disciples knew what had happened to the body. Where did it go? *Habeas corpus.* Show me the body.

To find the body, we need to start with the witnesses. The Christian faith rests upon eyewitness testimony, so it is important to hear out the witnesses. What did they do? Who are they? What level of credibility do they have?

To determine the path the Shroud might have taken over the centuries, we need to consult the witnesses who claim to have seen it.

Since Christ was killed during Passover, right before the Sabbath,[71] and his family were pious Jews, they would have to have waited to dress the body fully. That means they were forced to do only part of the burial ceremony on Good Friday.

In ancient Israel, women were charged with anointing the bodies of the deceased in preparation for burial. The women who tended to Jesus were Mary Magdalene, out of whom the Bible says Jesus cast seven demons,[72] Mary the mother of James, Salome, Joanna, and other unnamed women.[73] According to Luke's Gospel,

> It was the day of Preparation, and the sabbath was beginning. The women who had come with him from Galilee followed, and saw the tomb, and how his body was laid; then they returned, and prepared spices and ointments.
>
> On the Sabbath they rested according to the commandment.
>
> But on the first day of the week, at early dawn, they went to the tomb, taking the spices which they had prepared. And they found the stone rolled away from the tomb, but when they went in they did not find the body.[74]

The Gospel story of the discovery of the empty tomb has all the elements of credibility.

For example, it's Mary Magdalene who is there at the tomb. She would be a societal outcast. In first-century Israel, a woman's testimony wasn't taken at its word, as Josephus, a contemporary of the figures in the New Testament, makes clear. "But let not a single witness be credited," he writes, "but three, or two at the least, and those such whose testimony is confirmed by their good lives. But let not the testimony of women be admitted, on account of the levity and boldness of their sex."[75]

Having such low social standing (the standard at the time), Mary, in theory, wouldn't be considered a reliable witness. The authors of the Gospel would have been aware of the popular opinion on a woman's testimony and its legal status. If they were fabricating a story, therefore, they would have selected better witnesses to enhance its credibility.

It's important to note that the women, not the male apostles, were the first ones to discover the empty tomb.

The stones that were commonly used to seal most of the tombs at the time were square blocks.[76] The Gospels say this one had been rolled aside, which suggests that the stone was instead round. Still, even a round stone would have been incredibly difficult to move. Some estimate that the stone could have weighed multiple tons.[77]

It would have taken several able-bodied men to move it. The average woman back then was barely five feet tall.[78] It is very improbable that the women could have moved the stone by themselves.

One of the most stunning aspects of this scene is the absence of the guards. It is possible that the guards did not take the Pharisees' claims about the potential body snatchers seriously and simply fell asleep. We know that, if Roman guards fell asleep on duty, they would face the death penalty.[79] It is unlikely that they would have slacked off if their lives were on the line. As we'll see later in Matthew's Gospel, the chief priests assured the guards that they would speak highly of the guards to Pilate if he heard that the body went missing under their watch.

Some academics suggest that the story of the guard in Matthew was fictional and only an exercise in Christian apologetics.[80]

The Gospel of John reports that Mary Magdalene then rushed to report what she saw (or didn't see) to the disciples, who were hiding from the Jewish authorities in a safe location:

> Now on the first day of the week Mary Magdalene came to the tomb early, while it was still dark, and saw that the stone had been taken away from the tomb. So she ran, and went to Simon Peter and the other disciple, the one whom Jesus loved, and said to them, "They have taken the Lord out of the tomb, and we do not know where they have laid him."[81]

The disciples apparently didn't think Jesus would rise from the dead either.[82] It seems likely that they would also have feared that his body had been snatched in the middle of the night. Other key witnesses would be the apostles Peter and John. John writes that he saw the face cloth of Jesus. He saw the Shroud at the tomb. And there it is inscribed:

> Peter then came out with the other disciple, and they went toward the tomb. They both ran, but the other disciple outran Peter and reached the tomb first; and stooping to look in, he saw the linen cloths lying there, but he did not go in. Then Simon Peter came, following him, and went into the tomb; he saw the linen cloths lying, and the napkin, which had been on his head, not lying with the linen cloths but rolled up in a place by itself. Then the other disciple, who reached the tomb first, also went in, and he saw and believed; for as yet they did not know

> the scripture, that he must rise from the dead. Then the disciples went back to their homes.[83]

The Jewish authorities, according to Matthew's Gospel, spread rumors that the disciples stole the body, to discredit Jesus' followers' claims of a resurrection.

As the Jewish authorities would undoubtedly attest, the stakes were high. In life, Jesus had taken a sizable chunk out of their loyal following. If it could be proven that he rose from the dead, the rest of their power would dry up in the blink of an eye. St. Matthew tells us:

> While they were going, behold, some of the guard went into the city and told the chief priests all that had taken place. And when they had assembled with the elders and taken counsel, they gave a sum of money to the soldiers and said, "Tell people, 'His disciples came by night and stole him away while we were asleep.' And if this comes to the governor's ears, we will satisfy him and keep you out of trouble." So they took the money and did as they were directed; and this story has been spread among the Jews to this day.[84]

As previously noted, the tomb was not entirely empty. Jesus' burial cloths were still there. When the tomb was discovered, inside were the *othonia* mentioned in John's Gospel (19:40).[85] According to some scholars, *othonia* meant "a general assemblage of cloths."[86] Others say it means "strips of linen," which, if an accurate description of Jesus' burial cloths, would mean the Shroud was not legitimate.[87] The Synoptic Gospels mention that Joseph of Arimathea used a large, singular cloth, a sindon, to wrap Jesus. Luke's Gospel uses both; *sindon* at the taking down of Jesus from the cross and *othonia* to describe the cloths in the empty tomb.[88]

According to the Gospels, once the disciples saw the empty tomb, they believed. But what about the tomb made them believe? What made them think not that Jesus' body was stolen but that he had risen from the dead? Did they see a miraculous image of Jesus on the Shroud?

Each of the four Gospels mentions the burial cloth of Christ. Several verses mention that Jesus left behind multiple burial cloths. John mentions that there was a face cloth, separate from the other linens that were wrapped around Jesus' body.[89]

Jews would often wrap their deceased with a face cloth (as recounted in the Lazarus story) in addition to the much larger one that was wrapped around the whole body.[90]

This facecloth is the "napkin" mentioned in the passage above. Luke also reports on the cloths left behind in the tomb: "But Peter rose and ran to the tomb; stooping and looking in, he saw the linen cloths by themselves; and he went home wondering at what had happened."[91]

The Gospels report that after the disciples saw the empty tomb, Jesus appeared to them in their hiding place. They were shocked and feared that they were seeing a ghost.[92] Then Jesus revealed to them his wounds from the crucifixion, including the holes in his hands and the puncture wound in his side, and they all believed that he had risen from the dead.

The disciples went out and spread the news — blasphemy, according to the Jewish authorities. They would risk their lives by preaching that Jesus was the Son of God, and all but one of them would give up their lives for his sake.

But the threats did not stop the dissemination of the Christian message. Two thousand years later, billions of people believe the Gospel story of events regarding the mysterious resurrection of the controversial King of the Jews.

We have secular witnesses and believers in those first-century events of the death and so-called resurrection of the man called Jesus the Christ, the promised Messiah.

In terms of actual physical evidence of those events, all we know is that there were cloths that remained at the crime scene. They were taken somewhere and would eventually disappear from the written record.

Where did this King's Shroud — visual evidence of his suffering and, perhaps, resurrection — go? And would we hear of it again?

4

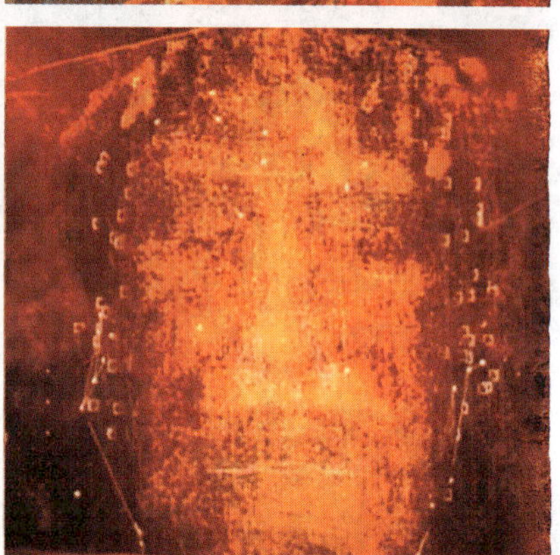

Shrouded by History

Though the King had left an indelible mark on his followers, his Shroud would be lost in the shadows of a dark age that was about to dawn — because once John's Gospel comes to a close, the trail of the Shroud goes cold. The Bible does not mention who (if anyone) took the linens out of the tomb or what they did with them.

In a way, that's not surprising. From the beginning, the "Jesus movement" was persecuted by the Jewish authorities in Israel, as evinced by the fate of its founder. Its leaders — the apostles — were making inroads across the known world, preaching and planting churches.

Everywhere they went, they were persecuted. Legend holds that nearly all the apostles were killed as martyrs (though St. John miraculously survived the attempt on his life).

What's more, Jesus died just forty years before the destruction of the Jewish Temple and the burning of various parts of Jerusalem, which happened during the rioting of the Jewish people against their pagan Roman rulers.[93]

There was massive unrest in the Christian homeland. One would assume, then, that disciples would make sure to protect such a crucial relic — key physical evidence of the resurrection, the basis of their Christian faith — even if it meant hiding the Shroud from the public.

Most of the disciples escaped Jerusalem before its final destruction. What were they going to take with them? It's likely they would want to keep relics of their risen God as close to them as possible. The most likely scenario is that the Shroud was removed from the Holy Land in or around AD 70 — the year Rome laid siege to Jerusalem and eventually wiped out virtually all Jewish presence in the city.[94]

A popular legend tells a different story. Supposedly, soon after the death of Jesus, the Shroud was taken out of Jerusalem by one of his apostles, Jude Thaddeus. He brought one of Jesus' burial cloths to King Abgar of Edessa, Syria. One version of this story comes from the early Church historian Eusebius.[95]

He says that Abgar was afflicted with leprosy and, having heard of Jesus' miraculous healings, wrote to implore him to come to Edessa to heal him. Jesus responded but did not come to Edessa. Instead, he commissioned his disciple, Thaddeus, to go in his place.

Not long after the resurrection, Thaddeus went to Edessa bearing a cloth with Jesus' likeness on it. Abgar venerated the cloth and, according to this legend, was healed of his leprosy. He converted to Christianity, as did many of his subjects. The faith flourished in Edessa until Abgar died.

His son, upon taking the throne, outlawed Christianity. Edessa's Christians had to take the Shroud with them into hiding.

Not until the Persians invaded was the Shroud rediscovered. Legend has it that the bishop of Edessa had a vision that led him to the Shroud, or what was then called the Image of Edessa, which was hidden in the walls of the city. At that moment, the tide of the war shifted, and the Persians were beaten back.[96]

Before the Image of Edessa, later called the Mandylion, was rediscovered in the sixth century, artistic depictions of Christ, or iconography, didn't reflect the image on the cloth, for obvious reasons. Some scholars say that you can see a clear change in Christian art once the image resurfaced.

Skeptics posit that while some paintings may reflect general similarities of the image of the man on the Shroud, the comparison is highly subjective and there are plenty of examples where the iconography differs from the image in the Shroud.[97]

Scholars who adhere to the inconographic theory posit that some Byzantine artists copied the image of the Mandylion, which they believed to be the face of Jesus. Paul Vignon, French artist and biologist, wrote a book in 1938 called *The Shroud of Turin: Science, Archaeology, History, Iconography, Logic,* in which he argues that the ancient depictions of Jesus were modeled after the man on the Shroud.[98]

An expert who has studied the Shroud of Turin for forty years makes the case that the Shroud image influenced art centuries before the Middle Ages:

> Professor Paul Vignon in the 1930s, [showed] an absolute and perfect correspondence between the iconography of Christ, which appeared as early as the end of the fourth century, and the face of the man on the Shroud. A change of iconographic model occurred at this time, which corresponds to the arrival of this precious linen in the city of Edessa, in present-day Turkey. It therefore seems impossible that a forgery could have been made in the Middle Ages, in the years 1260-1390—that is, the range provided by the radiocarbon laboratories.[99]

This is still more evidence that the cloth did not exist merely in legend.

The sixth and seventh centuries saw the rise of Islam. Muslim invaders took over Jerusalem circa 637. If the Shroud were still in the Middle East at this point, it would make sense that Christians in possession of the Shroud would feel the urgency to move their religious relic out of range of the religious wars.

In 944, the Image of Edessa arrived in Constantinople. The Byzantine emperor brokered a deal with Edessa's emir: he gave up Muslim prisoners and offered Edessa protection in exchange for the cloth.[100] Arab historians documented the image's arrival in the city.

Historians debate whether this was the same shroud that was later found in Turin or just one of many clever forgeries.[101] Or was this a face cloth that covered Jesus in the tomb?[102] There are, however, several historical accounts that claim that the Image of Edessa was, in fact, a full-body image of Jesus. They refer to it as "a cloth on which one can see not only a face but the whole body" and "the imprint . . . of the bodily appearance."[103]

Perhaps the absence of extensive records on the Shroud in Edessa can be explained by the Turks' invasion and ransacking of the Crusader-ruled city in 1144. Any icons or Christian religious symbols would have likely been destroyed.[104] Nonetheless, the historical record does show that a cloth believed by some to have covered Jesus Christ after the crucifixion appeared in Constantinople.

According to Dr. Gerard Verschuuren's acclaimed study of the Shroud:

> The writings of Arab historians verify that the city's emir had accepted a large sum of money from the Byzantine emperor in exchange for the Image.

But how do we know the cloth did arrive in Constantinople (which later became Istanbul after the Ottomans took over)? Thanks to a Rome classicist, Gino Zaninotto, we have access to a sermon from the Vatican Archives delivered by the archdeacon and referendary of Hagia Sophia, in the year 944. In the sermon, dated August 16, Archdeacon Gregory confirms the arrival of the Image of Edessa in Constantinople only one day before, thereby providing further reliable data as to its whereabouts.[105]

The cloth was renamed the Mandylion, the "handkerchief" or "towel" of Edessa.[106]

Over time, another cloth was rumored to be a burial cloth of Jesus. This one is called the Sudarium (or cloth) of Oviedo, which is housed at the Cathedral of San Salvador in Oviedo, Spain. Fr. Robert Spitzer, president of the Magis Institute, notes that the Sudarium's existence was documented as early as 616.[107] The cloth measures nearly thirty-three by twenty-one inches.[108] This could not be the cloth at Turin, which measures over fourteen feet long by three and a half feet wide.

So which is the real article: the Sudarium of Oviedo, the Mandylion, or the Shroud of Turin?

Recall that ancient Jewish burial shrouds often had two parts: the face cloth (or napkin) and the full-body cloth. It could be that the Sudarium of Oviedo might be one and the Shroud of Turin could be the other.

An analysis by Dr. Alan Whanger at Duke University found 120 points of coincidence between the face cloth of Oviedo and the blood stains on the Shroud.[109] This suggests that the same face left traces on two cloths. They were possibly the two burial cloths left behind in the tomb, as mentioned in John 20.

Nonetheless, the Sudarium disappeared around AD 944, but historical records suggest that the Shroud might have been in Constantinople during the twelfth century.

This brings us back tò the Mandylion. The big question is this: Why do the rumors and historical records of the Mandylion mention only an image of a man's face, not the rest of the body?

Some Shroud scholars, such as Ian Wilson, argue that the Mandylion is possibly the Shroud of Turin — just folded up. There are many reasons this might be the case, Wilson argues. For starters, there are clear fold marks on the Shroud, and the pattern indicates that the Shroud could have been folded up in such a way as to show only the face.[110] The Mandylion is referred to in the sixth century as a cloth doubled in four, or a tetradiplon.[111] Verschuuren claims that the term *tetradiplon* is used only twice in Greek texts, and both times it refers to the Mandylion.

If the Shroud was folded up, this could explain why there is no mention in the historical record of a full-body image of Jesus until the Middle Ages.

Purported drawings of the Shroud have been dated to around 1150. The sketch resembles the image of the man, not merely a face. The picture, drawn when the emperor of Constantinople invited foreign dignitaries to view the Shroud, detailed features that were unique to those of the man in the Shroud, along with burn marks that the linen had sustained from a fire in the chapel where the Shroud was housed at the time.[112]

In other words, this image most likely depicts the Shroud of Turin as we know it. This fact challenges the carbon-14 test, which dated the Shroud to only around 1260 to 1390.[113] Even if the Shroud is a forgery, it is still older than the carbon testing results suggested.

Evidence suggests that the Shroud was in Constantinople in the thirteenth century but was taken by the Crusaders during the Sack of Constantinople.

Less than a year before Constantinople was sacked, however, a crusader named Robert de Clari became one of the Shroud's first modern witnesses. After the sack of Constantinople, Clari wrote:

> And among those others there was another church which was called My Lady Saint Mary of Blachernae,

where there was the *sydoines* where our Lord had been wrapped, which every Friday raised itself upright, so that one could see the form of our Lord there; and no one, either Greek or French, ever knew what became of this sydoines when the city was taken.[114]

No one knows for sure what happened to the Image of Edessa after the Sack of Constantinople. There's a curious gap in the historical record of the Shroud between 1204 and the middle of the thirteenth century, when Geoffrey de Charny claimed possession of the Shroud. Meanwhile, are there any theories of what happened to the Shroud?

Some scholars believe the Crusaders brought it back West.[115] It is possible that the Knights Templar, a Christian military order formed to protect Christian pilgrims and the interests of the Crusaders, housed the Mandylion during this gap. Some historical documents indicate that part of the Templars' initiation rituals at that time involved the veneration of "a long linen cloth on which was impressed the figure of a man."[116]

Interestingly, the master of the Knights Templar in Normandy was named Geoffrey de Charnay. Was he related to the French knight Geoffrey de Charny, who publicized the Shroud in the 1300s? As Stevenson and Habermas note, it was common for the same surnames to have slight differentiations in spelling.[117]

Some hold that after the Crusades, the Shroud was transported to Athens, Greece, where it stayed until circa 1225 in the care of Otho IV de la Roche, a lord in Athens.[118] The details of the journey the Shroud took from Athens to France are murky.

In the historical record up to medieval times, there are a few instances of people claiming to have seen a mysterious or divine cloth with the image of a man's face imprinted on it. Some may have merit. But there are also many frauds.

The earliest mention in the historical record of the Shroud that is generally accepted as legitimate by scholars across the board dates back to France in the Middle Ages when, around 1357, a French knight called Geoffrey de Charny announced that he had come into possession of Christ's burial cloth.

Verschuuren says of Charny:

> He was the Lord of Lirey and a knight who died in the Battle of Poitiers in 1356. The first public exhibition of the Shroud, where it was shown at full length, occurred a year after his death and was sponsored by the canons of the Lirey cathedral. From then on, the news spread like wildfire. Large crowds of pilgrims came to see the cloth, believing that it carried the image of the crucified Jesus.[119]

It is important to know that Sir Geoffrey's wife, Jeanne de Vergy, was a relative of Otho de la Roche. The connection between the image in thirteenth-century Greece and the one that appears in fourteenth-century France is established.

Not all were convinced, however. In 1389, Pierre d'Arcis, bishop of Troyes, wrote to Pope Clement VII to inform him of the Shroud's inauthenticity:

> This could not be the real shroud of our Lord having the Saviour's Likeness thus imprinted upon it, since the holy Gospel made no mention of such an imprint, while, if it had been true, it was quite unlikely that the holy Evangelists

> would have omitted to record it or that the fact should have remained hidden until the present time.

In his memorandum, d'Arcis continued with a sentence that, to many, is the coup de grâce to the Shroud's authenticity, powerfully reinforcing the carbon dating result of 1988. According to Herbert Thurston's translation of d'Arcis's original Latin:

> Eventually, after diligent inquiry and examination, he [Henri of Poitiers] discovered the fraud and how the said cloth had been cunningly painted, the truth being attested by the artist who had painted it, to wit, that it was a work of human skill and not miraculously wrought or bestowed.[120]

Verschuuren explains:

> This verdict was perhaps understandable because, at the time, forgery of precious relics was rather common, and the bishop concluded that the Shroud was yet another case. Nevertheless, his verdict testifies to the fact that a burial cloth matching the description of the Shroud was indeed physically present in Lirey.[121]

In 1453, Margaret de Charny transferred the Shroud to the House of Savoy. The Shroud moved around with the Savoys but eventually settled in Chambéry, France. In 1532, a fire broke out in the chapel where the relic was housed.[122] The survival of the linen is often described as miraculous.[123]

Eventually, in 1578, Duke Emmanuel Philibert of the Savoy dynasty moved the relic to Turin, Italy. And there it remained, virtually untouched, until photographer Secondo Pia came along in 1898. Pia was the first photographer to see the Shroud, and he couldn't believe what his pictures revealed.

5

The Accidental Photograph

Secondo Pia was born in Asti, Piedmont, in 1855. An attorney by trade, he was deeply interested in both art and science, and in the early 1870s, he began to explore a new branch of both disciplines: photography. In the 1890s, he became a city councilor as well as a member of Turin's Amateur Photographers' Club.[124]

Pia is considered a pioneer in photography for using electric light bulbs in the 1890s, given that light bulbs were a novelty in the nineteenth century: Thomas Edison's incandescent bulb was invented only in 1879. But it was by accident that Secondo Pia unwittingly took the first step in the field of modern sindonology.[125]

In 1898, Turin was selected to host an Italian arts and culture festival, the Esposizione Generale Italiana. The Catholic community in Turin concurrently hosted their own festival, an exposition of Catholic arts and culture.[126] As part of the celebration, a sacred-art exhibition was planned.

The head of the Shroud Commission, Baron Manno, petitioned the king for a public display of the Shroud of Turin and asked for the right to photograph the cloth to promote the exhibition. The king agreed. Naturally, Secondo Pia was named the official photographer.

In the days leading up to the exhibition, Pia took the first photographs of the Shroud. This in itself was an achievement! But when he began to develop the black-and-white negatives, he couldn't believe what he had discovered.

His clever use of light, combined with the high-contrast image rendered by the negative, showed that the Shroud was infinitely more detailed — and vastly more lifelike — than anyone had realized. It showed a stunningly detailed image of a crucified man, with whippings, gashes on the skull and forehead where a crown of thorns could have been, a cut in the side of the ribcage, and nail wounds in the wrists.

Pia was astounded.[127] That one photograph alone galvanized the scientific community and gave heart to Christians. The news of the image, now considered by many believers to be proof positive of Christ's resurrection, spread like wildfire, and the image was reprinted around the world. Cheryl White, co-host of the podcast *Who Is the Man of the Shroud?*, notes that this photo "launched the age of Shroud science."[128]

In a 1973 televised address, Pope Paul VI recounted his first sight of the Shroud image, calling it "so true, so profound, so human and so divine, such as we have been unable to admire and venerate in any other image."[129]

Secondo Pia was well respected, but he would have his naysayers. Rumors spread that Pia doctored the image to make it look like Jesus. He was eventually vindicated when, decades later, another photographer, Giuseppe Enrie, was able to replicate the image that Pia captured.[130]

Pia's photo found its way into the hands of a nonbeliever named Yves Delage, who delivered a paper for the French Academy of Sciences examining the pathologies of the man of the Shroud and comparing them to what we know about the historical Jesus of Nazareth.[131]

He concluded that the man in the image is Jesus of Nazareth, becoming the first distinguished scientist to verify the Shroud's authenticity.

Delage did not make any faith claims. He was not a religious zealot. He had no ulterior motive for affirming the Shroud.

Still, the Academy would not publish his paper in the Academy's minutes unless he expunged the references to Jesus.[132] Delage was laughed out of the scientific community and wrote his colleagues to challenge their mockery, which was fueled by anti-religious sentiment.

Other non-Christian experts came to trust in the veracity of the image on the Shroud that Pia exposed. Photographer Leo Vala, an agnostic, went on record to say that he did not doubt that the image Pia captured was real:

> I've been involved in the invention of many complicated visual processes and I can tell you that no one could have faked that image. No one could do it today with the technology we have. . . . It's a perfect negative. It has a photographic quality that is extremely precise.[133]

The well-respected French surgeon Pierre Barbet wrote a book on the Shroud, in which he analyzed the pathologies of the man in the image that showed up on Pia's image. He agreed that Pia's negative showed an incredibly detailed image of what could be described only as a crucified man. The details conform not only to the traditional account of Jesus' crucifixion, but to an anatomically correct version of a crucified body.

According to Verschuuren, Barbet "declared the anatomical conditions of the man in the Shroud authentic and the wounds consistent with those of crucified victims. Barbet, who had done fifteen years of medical research on the image of the Shroud of Turin, described the physiology and pathology of the crucified man on the Shroud as 'almost perfect from the anatomical point of view.' "[134]

Barbet was astounded at the anatomically perfect image on the Shroud. The blood flow, the placement of the wounds — it all squared with the science.

As Verschuuren notes, other scientists have weighed in on the anatomy of the Shroud image:

> A second opinion came from Frederick Zugibe, professor of pathology at Columbia University Vagelos College of Physicians and Surgeons. In order to verify the anatomical conditions of a crucified person, the professor suspended himself and other volunteers from crosses and noted the physiological responses. In his 1998 book, Zugibe also authenticated the image on the Shroud but presented alternative judgements on various details outlined by Barbet's study.[135]

Zugibe determined that the bloodstains accurately portray a man who was wounded while he was in the vertical position but also reflects how the blood would have dripped once he was laid down horizontally.

Pia's photo revealed a much clearer image of the face on the Shroud — one that allowed for a clearer understanding of how pre-medieval artists likely used the Shroud image as a template for their depictions of Jesus.

We can compare the face of the man of the Shroud with the icons that have been painted throughout history, even going back to the Mandylion.

As mentioned earlier, the Shroud wasn't well known before the sixth century. The early portrayals of Christ showed a short-haired, beardless man. Scholars believe that this is because the iconographers tended to be Roman; their depictions of Jesus were rendered with the characteristics with which those artists were most familiar. So at first, Jesus seemed to have a rounded face.

Then, around the time the Image of Edessa (re)surfaced, there was a revolution in Christian art. Jesus suddenly had the long, bearded face of a Semite. Other facial features unique to the Shroud image were also in those artistic renditions of Jesus, which included a wisp of hair on the forehead, accentuated cheeks, and round eyes.

The face of Jesus seen in two sixth-century pieces of art, the icon Christ Pantocrator and a vase with a depiction of Jesus, is strikingly similar to the face on the Shroud.

Even particular marks on the face of the man in the Shroud come out in the Byzantine iconography.[136] In the Turin image, we see a line across the throat — a line that appears over and over again in these antique paintings. One ancient image shows a scar above Jesus' nose, his raised eyebrows, and some of the contusions around his cheekbones — wounds that appear quite clearly on the Shroud.

The images have a stunning number of points of congruence or visual similarities.[137] When we compare many of these medieval paintings with the Shroud, we find some points of coincidence. One painting from the sixth century may have as many as 250 points of coincidence with the Shroud of Turin.[138]

Some have asked how these early painters were able to copy the image, given that it was only in 1898 that one could see these details, thanks to Pia's photograph. Again, the answer is deceptively simple. It's possible that the image on the Shroud diminished over time, as the fabric yellowed and the contrast between the darker body image and the white cloth behind it was reduced.

In the 1970s, researchers at Duke University, including Dr. Alan Whanger and his wife, Mary, enhanced the eyes of the man on the

Shroud by a process using photographic enlargement and computer processing. The results seemed to show that there were coins resting on the eyelids. When the image was enlarged, it was determined that the coins were minted in the time of Pontius Pilate and dated back to AD 29.

Dr. Francis Filas at the University of Chicago Loyola also studied the coin images. He was convinced that his findings showed that the mysterious images over the eyelids were Roman lepton coins that he could date back to Jesus' time.[139] Although analyses from multiple scientists have reached the same conclusion that these are Roman coins from the first century, a reasonable amount of skepticism still exists in the scientific community.

Barrie Schwortz, official documenting photographer on the Shroud of Turin Research Project (STURP), casts doubt on the reliability of the methods used to analyze the image of the eyelids on the Shroud:

> My personal opinion, based on my photographic experience and my close examination of the Shroud itself, is that the weave of the cloth is far too coarse to resolve the rather subtle and very tiny inscription on a dime sized ancient coin. I believe the fibers are much too large to resolve such fine detail. Also, Filas found these coin "images" on the Shroud using the 1933 Enrie photographs. He personally mentioned to me that he could not achieve the same results with the 1978 photographs. Unfortunately, the 1933 photographs have been copied and recopied multiple times and I believe the "images" he discovered are artifacts of clumped photographic

> grain, caused by the recopying and enhancement of grain structure from earlier generation photographs. This grain clumping is very common on high contrast or contrast enhanced films when copied over multiple generations.[140]

The Whangers claim that, in the 1980s and 1990s, they identified on the Shroud an image of several flowers and plant leaves (possibly from a funeral bouquet) that are found in Israel.

Their findings confirm those of a Swiss criminologist named Max Frei. In 1978, during STURP's investigation, Frei used sticky tape to collect samples of pollen from the surface of the Shroud. He claimed that the pollen he collected originated from several places along the alleged path of the Shroud, including Chambéry, Lirey, and even Israel. He claimed that traces from all the relevant sites were found on the cloth.

In fact, three-quarters of the pollen grains that Frei identified are allegedly from around Judea. He claimed that around fifteen of the pollens are not found outside that region.

The second-largest number of pollen grains he identified were from Edessa, Turkey, where the Mandylion was rumored to be. Pollens local to the Constantinople region were also identified on the Shroud.[141]

Although there are those who believe in the veracity of Frei's claims, others familiar with his work question both the integrity of his methods and the reliability of such pollen samples to retrace the path of the Shroud accurately.[142] Shroud scholar Andrea Nicolotti notes a significant problem with Frei's studies:

> An accusation against Frei was lodged by a sindonologist who was a friar who had gained close knowledge of the photographs of the magnified

pollens that Frei used to show during his lectures. The friar correctly asserted that the photographs did not portray pollens of the species declared to be present on the Shroud. This gave rise to suspicions of fraud.[143]

Both the Whangers and Frei identified the same types of plants: flowers only found in the Holy Land.[144] The cloth itself was woven in a way that some claim was done in Galilee, in Judea.[145]

How could a medieval forger have collected these samples? And why would he have bothered? Why include "evidence" that no one in his own time could ever detect, much less verify? The Shroud's detractors so far have no answer.

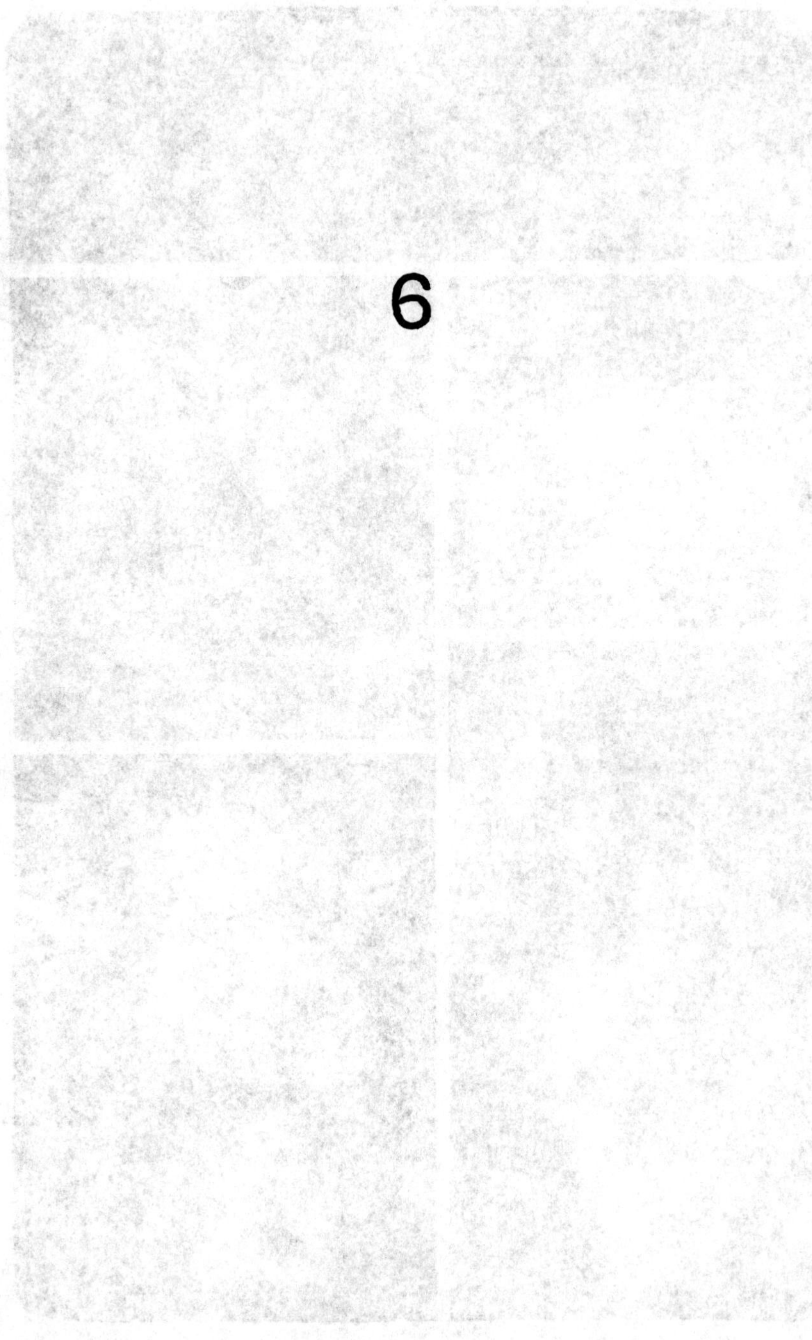
6

Case of the Evil Genius

After the release of Secondo Pia's negative of the Shroud image, many believed that the photo supported the theory that the Shroud was the authentic burial cloth of Jesus. It appeared that science and religion had reconciled in the event. The image baffled scientists as they grasped for natural explanations for the Shroud phenomenon.

But Pia's extraordinary image also galvanized the skeptics, making their efforts to debunk the Shroud feel all the more urgent. Despite the evidence, many still claim that the Shroud has medieval origins. They even claim to have succeeded (at least partially) in recreating the image.

For instance, some critics have argued that the Shroud was created by "reenacting" Jesus' burial using a model—probably a dead one. For instance, a corpse would be given wounds like the ones Jesus was recorded to have received in the biblical account of his crucifixion, then a shroud would be draped over the body to absorb the bloodstains.

This would explain the genuine marks on the linens and the anatomically accurate image of a crucified man.

Some of the proponents of this theory claim that Leonardo da Vinci was the architect of the reenactment in the fifteenth or sixteenth century. Over his lifetime, da Vinci dissected around thirty corpses as subjects for his artistic depictions of the human form.[146] Would it be far out of the realm of possibility, then, that a genius artist such as da Vinci also figured out a way to create the image on the Shroud?

It at least seems plausible that a corpse could be used to create the bloodstains on the linen. The catch is, to re-create the image that we see on the Shroud today, da Vinci first would have had to utilize an advanced form of photography to apply the image — technology that, of course, would not exist for centuries.[147]

Another theory popular among skeptics is that the image was an artist's rendition of the crucified Jesus. Medieval forgeries were a dime a dozen, so at first blush, this is a plausible hypothesis. Some point out that this could explain the curious gap in the historical record of a miraculous cloth of the risen Christ.

Emanuela Marinelli and Marco Fasol, proponents of the Shroud's authenticity, identify the chemist Walter McCrone as one of the foremost scholarly advocates of this theory. McCrone identified iron oxide and mercury sulphide on the surface of the Shroud, both of which are used in fake blood.[148]

Marinelli and Fasol claim that McCrone's findings have since been refuted by two Shroud scientists who determined that the iron oxide McCrone uncovered was not present on the cloth.

What's more, scientists have determined that the image is only on the surface. It does not bleed through to deeper levels of the linen. Therefore, whatever created the image on the Shroud doesn't behave the way paint does, as shown by the image on the herringbone weave.[149]

Whether the weave pattern is evidence in favor of an authentic Shroud is debatable. When examined up close, the herringbone pattern is a very intricate weave, and thus would have been at the very least rare in ancient times.[150]

Most baffling of all, though, is that the image of Turin could not have been made by paint because it contains no pigments. It has no real color as such.

Some have even tried using sand to scrape a fine image (like the one on the Shroud) onto a swatch of linen. These experiments have been unsuccessful because of the cloth's loose net weave. In other words, the impression created by the sand is still too shallow to have been made by sand. As with paint, the grains of sand would have gone right through the mesh to the other side, whereas the Shroud image is on one side and barely on the surface.

Other scientists prefer the vapor theory as an explanation for the image on the Shroud. Theoretically, it would allow for the image of a man crucified and covered in oils to be transferred onto a cloth. The theory is that the image came from vapors emanating from Jesus' body. Along with the vapors, the urea from the blood and sweat would have mixed with the aloes and spices on the skin to create an imprint on the Shroud.[151]

First, according to the biblical testimony, Jesus' family and friends could not have applied many of the burial aloes in their rush to leave the tomb before the Sabbath began.[152] They probably quickly laid the body in the tomb without washing it.

Second, vapors dissipate as they move through any kind of atmosphere that is not resistant. They begin to spread indiscriminately. Anyone who has ever boiled a pot of water knows that.

Shroud researchers Marinelli and Fasol put this refutation in more scientific terms:

> But it must be noticed that the vapor diffusion is never orthogonal, but it is straight in every direction; moreover the quantity of sweat present on the body was not evenly distributed

> and sufficient to determine such an extended and homogeneous imprint that exists on the Shroud.
>
> The skin of the corpse tends to be acid, not alkaline; besides in Vignon's hypothesis, there should be a difference between the dorsal imprint and the frontal one, but on the contrary, [it] does not exist in the Shroud's image. The research performed by American scientists points to another obstacle with this theory, the ammonia vapors would have penetrated throughout the cloth, while the image is only superficial.[153]

What's more — and once again — the image is simply too "shallow" to have been made by vapor. The residue would have penetrated the middle of the fiber. Instead, no traces are found in the middle of the cloth, nor does it penetrate beyond the very first layer of fibers.

These and many other methods were proposed by skeptics to challenge the Shroud's authenticity, which is why the Shroud of Turin Research Project (STURP) team was able to know exactly what to look for when they analyzed the Shroud. They knew what to rule out.

Before STURP submitted its findings in the late 1970s, the theory that the image was possibly burned or scorched onto the linen was possibly the most widely held theory to explain the Shroud.[154]

> [A] scorch could exhibit many of the characteristics present on the Shroud, such as oxidation, dehydration, and conjugation of linen fibrils, superficiality, the absence of saturation or image plateaus, and thermal and water stability and coloration. In other words, a scorch explains such phenomena as the conditions of the image fibrils themselves, the fact that this

> image is on the surface fibrils only, and that there are no points at which the image soaks into the cloth (except for the blood stains). A scorch can also account for the coloring and the resistance of the image to changes brought about by heat or water.

Tests seemed to show that certain physical qualities of the image matched those of the burn marks that the linen acquired from the chapel fire in 1532. STURP's 1978 study found, however, that the fibers on the Shroud are not burned or melted together, despite the obvious fire damage sustained in the chapel fire. To quote Marinelli and Fasol:

> It is scientifically proven that heat was not the mechanism used to create the Shroud image, demonstrated from the UV fluorescence photograph taken in 1978, by Veron Miller. The burned linen reacts under specific UV light. The whole Shroud was photographed with special lights and UV filters. The resulting photographs showed clearly fluorescence in all the burning and scorching areas on the Shroud, but absolutely no fluorescence in the image area. This test indicates that heat has been definitively ruled out as a mechanism of image formation.[155]

STURP also reported that the blood was present on the Shroud before the image was created — however exactly it was created. X-ray analysis of the Shroud confirms their finding. There is no dehydration of the cloth underneath the blood stains, which means that the blood got there first and then the image came second.

A painter would have put the image on before letting the blood drip on. Otherwise, how would he know exactly how to space blood spots to correspond to the wounds? And, again, if the image were a forgery, why would an artist bother with such details — ones that could be neither verified nor disproven for hundreds of years?

What's more, fluorescing tests showed that there was no scorching of the cloth beyond where the actual stains were from the fire in Chambéry. These scorchings are not anywhere near the body.[156]

One of the leaders of STURP, John Jackson, has even posited that several of the stains could have been made by food, corroborating another theory that the Shroud could have been present at the Last Supper.[157] It could have been one of two tablecloths. Sometimes the Jews would use two tablecloths, one under the food and another to put on top of the dishes to prevent bugs from getting to the leftover food. Now, what is called the Holy Tablecloth is at the Cathedral of Coria in Spain. The Shroud may have been the other tablecloth.

Another very popular theory held by modern physicists is that the image was produced by some form of radiation.

According to a research paper prepared by Mark Antonacci, president of the Test the Shroud Foundation, particle radiation "could account for or explain all of the primary and secondary body image features, the excellent condition of the cloth, its back side imaging, its possible flower and coin images, and the still red color of the centuries-old blood."[158]

No other scientific theory presented thus far seemed to be able to address the image of the Shroud. According to Marinelli and Fasol:

> Biophysicist Jean-Baptiste Rinaudo, researcher of nuclear medicine in Montpellier, carried out an interesting experiment. According to Rinaudo, the acid oxidizing of the superficial fibrils

> of the Shroud in the image areas, the tridimensional information contained in the figure and the vertical projection of the points that form the imprint can be explained with a radiation of protons that would have been given out of the body, under the effect of a contribution of unknown energy.[159]

They continue:

> At the ENEA (Ente per le Nuove tecnologie, l'Energia e l'Ambiente: Institution for the New Technologies, Energy, and Environment) of Frascati (Rome), a group of physicists carried out very important experiments. Some linen cloths have been irradiated with an excimer laser that emits a UV radiation at a high intensity. The results, confronted with the Shroud image, show interesting analogies: the coloring is similar, and it is limited to the superficial part of the cloth. It is confirmed in this way the possibility that the Shroud image has been provoked by a directional UV radiation. The coloring of the linen becomes more intense as time passes.[160]

If one were to fabricate the light that created the image, one would need a very bright light indeed. If the ultraviolet-light-radiation hypothesis were true, it would take between six and eight billion watts of light energy for one forty-billionth of a second. The forger would need roughly fourteen thousand argon fluoride excimer lasers to create such an image.[161] That's nearly half a million searchlights' worth of light energy—all emitted at the same time, at the same moment, in the exact shape and likeness of a man matching the description of Jesus of Nazareth. This is something we can't even imagine doing in the twenty-first century. For a medieval forger, it would be impossible.

No one has ever been able to explain how the image was applied to the linen — at least, not in terms a scientist would accept. No one has successfully replicated the image. Gary Habermas and Kenneth Stevenson identified this as the glaring holes in skeptics' arguments:

> Naturalistic hypotheses that would account for the Shroud must explain at least (a) the absence of decomposition, (b) the fact that the body was apparently not unwrapped when it separated from the cloth, and (c) a very possible light or heat scorch from (d) a dead body in a state of rigor mortis. Theories involving an unwrapped, rewrapped, or stolen body are confounded by (b) and (c). Those claiming that the person in question never died are disproved by (b), (c), and (d). Most other naturalistic theories are refuted by one or more of these phenomena.[162]

After considering the alternative explanations of how the detailed image of a tortured and crucified man was put onto the Shroud, the likeliest answer seems to be that a large amount of radiation created the image. But where would such a light come from?

7

A 3-D Image and a False Carbon Test?

In 1976, a group of researchers at Sandia Laboratories used a VP-8 Image Analyzer to scrutinize Giuseppe Enrie's 1931 photograph of the man in the Shroud.[163] They were shocked to discover that the image of the face in the photograph contained three-dimensional information that allowed the imager to create an accurate topographic image of the man's face.[164]

"When the Shroud's negative image was placed beneath the machine," researcher Ian Wilson, recounts, "the result was nothing short of astonishing. A consistent 'true' 3D effect was produced . . . around which it was possible, via the device's TV monitor, to move, viewing the contours of the body just as if viewing a range of mountains from a moving helicopter."[165]

As the physician Frederick Zugibe explains, a simple painting could not contain the multidimensional qualities STURP discovered on the Shroud image:

> They obtained dazzling, tridimensional photos of the Shroud image, which they indicate is not

> possible with regular photography because the latter would show distortion with flattening of the relief including the arm within the chest and nose pressed into face. They also observed that, because the image produced no directional brush stroke marks such as might have been effected by an artist, forgery did not appear possible.[166]

This discovery shocked many in the scientific community. Peter Schumacher, a designer of the VP-8, described his reaction to the full-body image the analyzer produced:

> A "true three-dimensional image" appeared on the monitor. . . . The nose ramped in relief. The facial features were contoured properly. Body shapes of the arms, legs and chest and the basic human form. . . . I had never heard of the Shroud of Turin before that moment. I had no idea what I was looking at. However, the results are unlike anything I have processed through the VP-8 Image Analyzer, before or since. Only the Shroud of Turin has [ever] produced these results from a VP-8 Image Analyzer.[167]

Schumacher addressed the skeptics' claims that the Shroud was a clever forgery:

> One must consider how and why an artist would embed three-dimensional information in the "grey" shading of an image [when] no means of viewing this property of the image would be available for at least 650 years after this was done. One would have to ask why is this result

> not obtained in the analysis of other works? . . . Why would the artist make only one such work requiring such special skills and talent, and not pass the technique along to others? How could the artist control the quality of the work when he or she could not "see" grey scale as elevation? . . . Would an artist produce this work before the device to show the results was [even] invented?[168]

So much controversy, and so many unanswered questions, call out for an official investigation. Enter STURP.

The Shroud of Turin Research Project was a team of more than two dozen highly qualified chemists, photographers, physicists, biophysicists, computer scientists and other experts who led the first major research project on the Shroud.[169]

Contrary to the kneejerk assumptions of many skeptics, the group consisted of "a very small number of devout believers, a scattering of agnostics, with a majority of not particularly devout or convinced believers." One biophysicist even did a headcount: "Six agnostics, two Mormons, three Jews, four Roman Catholics, 'and an assortment of Methodists, Lutherans, Congregationalists, Episcopalians, and Dutch Reformed.' "

The coordinator of the group even said, "As far as I was concerned, science was my God."[170]

They asked the then owner of the Shroud, King Umberto II, the Duke of Savoy, for five days of unfettered access to the Shroud so they could conduct nonstop, round-the-clock study. They spent a year preparing for the tests, carefully planning out their limited time with the Shroud. They conducted a massive amount of tests on the linen, from X-rays to fluorescence and microchemistry tests; they wanted as thorough an investigation as possible into the Shroud.

Who knew when they would have another chance to analyze the most prized relic in the world?

The STURP analysis unveiled much critical information about the Shroud. X-Ray analysis showed that the supposed bloodstains did not contain lead paint, suggesting that these were truly bloodstains, not an artist's rendition. Further analysis conducted with ultraviolet photography did not detect any brush strokes on the linens.[171] The evidence in favor of the Shroud's being Jesus' burial cloth was piling up.

STURP took a light sample of the debris and other particles on the Shroud and brought in two additional authorities to study them: the chemist Dr. John Heller and the blood chemist Dr. Alan Adler. Their analyses corroborated that the apparent bloodstains were not painted on. Ian Wilson notes that the stains "passed eleven different diagnostic tests that would allow them to be pronounced as true blood in any court of law."[172]

These findings were presented in the final summary of the group's research. Heller concluded in the press release:

> No pigments, paints, dyes or stains have been found on the fibrils. X-ray, fluorescence and microchemistry on the fibrils preclude the possibility of paint being used as a method for creating the image. Ultra Violet and infrared evaluation confirm these studies. Computer image enhancement and analysis by a device known as a VP-8 image analyzer show that the image has unique, three-dimensional information encoded in it. Microchemical evaluation has indicated no

> evidence of any spices, oils, or any biochemicals known to be produced by the body in life or in death. It is clear that there has been a direct contact of the Shroud with a body, which explains certain features such as scourge marks, as well as the blood. However, while this type of contact might explain some of the features of the torso, it is totally incapable of explaining the image of the face with the high resolution that has been amply demonstrated by photography.[173]

Heller went on to announce that none of the scientists in the group could explain the image on the Shroud. No branch of modern science represented on the STURP team held the answers as to how the image was created. Heller concluded:

> However, there are no chemical or physical methods known which can account for the totality of the image, nor can any combination of physical, chemical, biological or medical circumstances explain the image adequately.
>
> Thus, the answer to the question of how the image was produced or what produced the image remains, now, as it has in the past, a mystery.
>
> We can conclude for now that the Shroud image is that of a real human form of a scourged, crucified man. It is not the product of an artist. The blood stains are composed of hemoglobin and also give a positive test for serum albumin. The image is an ongoing mystery and until further chemical studies are made, perhaps by this group

of scientists, or perhaps by some scientists in the future, the problem remains unsolved.[174]

No one can explain the image on the Shroud or re-create the image with technology or even come up with a plausible scientific theory as to how (or why) the image was transferred onto the cloth in the first place.

The next major study to be conducted on the Shroud was the long-awaited carbon-14 dating test. Many believers in the Shroud's authenticity wanted a dating test to be done on the Shroud. Pia's astonishing photograph, the blood on the linen, the STURP findings — all of this pointed to the cloth's authenticity.

The momentum and seemingly the science were in favor of an authentic Shroud.

In 1988, the British Museum and the Holy See commissioned three labs to conduct a carbon-14 test on the Shroud. The labs were at Oxford University, the University of Arizona, and the Swiss Federal Institute of Criminology. Even in the 1980s, carbon-14 dating was a relatively accurate and trusted method of dating ancient archaeological objects.

A year of preparation went into the study, but finally in 1988, they cut away from the Shroud a strip of eight centimeters. They split it in two and held half in reserve. The cloth was cut from the Shroud judiciously, as the carbon dating tests would destroy the sample.

The carbon-14 dating process involves carbonization, in which the testers burn the sample and then count the molecules that are there. Then they compare how much carbon-14 there is in relation to carbon-12.

Half of the strip was divided among the three laboratories. The samples were not, however, split evenly; Arizona's piece was smaller than the rest, so the lab got a second snippet called Arizona Two. So, in the end, four individual samples were tested.

The results were publicized in October 1988. The final report from the labs conducting the test did not deliver the expected results. The labs dated the material to 1260 to 1390, "with a confidence of 95 percent accuracy."[175]

The announcement devastated those who were certain that the Shroud was the burial cloth of Jesus. Carbon dating is considered the gold standard for age-testing organic materials. At first glance, the results look damning.

And yet ever since the original report of the findings was published in the renowned scientific magazine *Nature*, some in the scientific community have doubted that the original report is as conclusive as it was made out to be.[176] There are now several objections to the carbon-14 report that have merit and require serious consideration.

It is likely safe to assume that the laboratories were competent and completed the carbon dating tests accurately. Even so, the section of the Shroud that they tested has been shown to be questionable at best. The labs appeared to test an anomalous portion of the Shroud.

What's more, experts knew it to be anomalous ten years prior to the testing.

The STURP investigation revealed that different parts of the Shroud were different ages. A simple brightness map showed that the chemical composition of the Shroud was the same throughout — except for the top-left corner. Yet that is where they cut away the sample to be tested.[177]

According to the original protocols, there would be seven samples from different areas of the Shroud. That later was reduced to three, then one.

Fr. Andrew Dalton notes that the seven labs were supposed to work independently of each other and would likewise each publish its findings separately. In the end, there was only one report that combined the results of the experiments of the three labs.[178] Once Zurich, Arizona, and Oxford were selected, the directors of these three labs insisted that more labs be involved in testing the Shroud. This, they assured the archbishop of Turin, would ensure the accuracy of the test results. Nonetheless, despite the urging of the labs, no more testing facilities were allowed to conduct carbon-14 dating on the Shroud.[179]

Andrea Nicolotti, a renowned historian and skeptic of the Shroud's authenticity, notes that there were some notable irregularities in how the dating study was conducted. Usually, Nicolotti notes, samples meant to be carbon dated are sent out to labs without letting the labs know what the sample is. In this case, however, it was a public affair. Labs competed to get to test the renowned and controversial Shroud of Turin. Nicolotti argues that in the case of the Shroud, the dating process, considered to be routine and straightforward, was overhyped and over-publicized, creating the false impression that dating was more complicated and sensitive than it was.

What's more, the late Raymond Rogers, who was a chemist from the Los Alamos National Laboratory in New Mexico, claimed that through testing a chemical called vanillin in the Shroud samples the 1988 team used for the carbon-14 tests, he determined that the Shroud must be older than the carbon-14 dating results determined.[180]

Fr. Robert Spitzer remarks that several other dating methods have been tried on the Shroud and that those tests, when their results are averaged together, date the Shroud centuries older than the carbon test allowed for. Those tests, including the vanillin test, suggest that the Shroud could have originated from the first century AD.[181]

The British Museum refused to release the full report of the accumulated carbon dating tests, despite multiple requests for them to do so. It wasn't until 2017 that the results were released via a Freedom of Information request.[182]

Tristan Casabianca, the researcher who filed the request, along with a group of scientists and Shroud researchers, including Emanuela Marinelli, Giuseppe Pernagallo, and Benedetto Torrisi, concluded that the 1988 dating test results were misleading.[183] Their findings were published in *Archaeometry*, a peer-reviewed academic journal at the University of Oxford.

Casabianca argues that the sample of the Shroud was not representative of the whole cloth, which measures more than fourteen feet long and more than three and a half feet wide. The sample, taken from the edge, was likely from a repaired section of the linen that was sewn due to wear and tear from being handled over the centuries.[184]

The samples used for carbon-14 dating may have been contaminated with cotton fibers that were added to the Shroud in the Middle Ages.[185] The edges may have also been cut off for believers to use as relics.[186]

As we know, the Shroud was burned in 1532 by a fire that broke out in the chapel where it was being housed in Chambéry, France. The linen was also stained by melted silver from the case in which the Shroud had been placed.

The damaged edges were likely repaired with dyed cotton and a stitching method known as "invisible mending."[187] More scientists and scholars now hold that this is the area from which the carbon-14 dating sample was taken.

"The tested samples are obviously heterogeneous (many different dates), and there is no guarantee that all these samples, taken from one end of the sheet (Shroud), are representative of the whole fabric. It is therefore impossible to conclude that the Shroud of Turin dates from the Middle Ages," Casabianca said.[188]

He notes that the results of the carbon dating test are not "conclusive," as they were originally proclaimed to be. These new findings open a new chapter in the study of the Shroud.

The raw data published by Casabianca and his fellow researchers indicated that the first Arizona sample, Arizona One, dates to around 1240 but that Arizona Two (which was located around two centimeters to the right of the first sample) is two hundred years younger.

How could this be? Was there something wrong with the method of dating that the scientists employed in 1988? Calling attention to this seeming irregularity, Fr. Dalton notes that if this trend continued and the Shroud kept getting younger the farther one moved to the right, then that would mean that parts of the Shroud would have to date far into the future (which is obviously absurd).[189]

These results inspire reasonable doubt in the original conclusion of the labs' report. The results showing the major age discrepancies in the cloth's materials were buried under the rather excited headlines at the time that claimed that the carbon dating test definitively proved that the Shroud is a fake.

Casabianca and his colleagues concluded that another carbon dating test would need to be done to determine the true age of the Shroud:

> The measurements made by the three laboratories on the TS [Turin Shroud] sample suffer from a lack of precision which seriously affects the reliability of the 95% AD 1260-1390 interval. The statistical analyses, supported by the foreign material found by the laboratories, show the necessity of a new radiocarbon dating to compute a new reliable interval.[190]

The scientists in the STURP investigation pressed tape all over the Shroud, documenting where they took the samples. Fr. Spitzer claimed that those tape samples show cotton fibers in the spot precisely where the samples were taken for the carbon-14 dating tests.

If Casabianca's conclusions are correct, then the issue of the age of the Shroud is far from settled science. The case has been reopened. We are back to the drawing board.

Why don't we just have one more carbon-14 dating test to clear up the confusion?

Pope John Paul II encouraged the scientific community to continue to test the Shroud. In a May 1988 address, commemorating Pia's photo of the Shroud, he said:

> Since it is not a matter of faith, the Church has no specific competence to pronounce on these questions. She entrusts to scientists the task of continuing to investigate, so that satisfactory answers may be found to the questions connected with this Sheet, which, according to tradition, wrapped the body of our Redeemer after he had been taken down from the cross. The Church urges that the Shroud be studied without pre-established positions that take for granted results that are not such; she invites them to act with interior freedom and attentive respect for both scientific methodology and the sensibilities of believers.[191]

It seems clear why some would be hesitant to try the test again, after the politics and drama the first time around. They want things to be done right. It would also likely take an international consensus from the scientific community to cut up the Shroud again.

Still, the Shroud does not have to be carbon dated. There are alternative methods of testing that might be able to date the Shroud more accurately. Carbon dating has been hailed as the "gold standard" of dating organic material, but the Shroud is unique in that its exposure to fire and the likelihood that some of the material has been replaced since the Middle Ages could compromise the accuracy of a carbon-14 test.[192] If the image were applied to the Shroud through radiation, this would likewise render carbon dating ineffective. The carbon dating could be inaccurate if nuclear disintegration (a "minor nuclear explosion" in which "light and energy would also be produced"[193]) was the method by which the image came onto the Shroud.

Using radiation, scientists would need to search for the cosmogenic nuclear isotopes in the Shroud. If scientists can confirm that there is a high proportion of chlorine 36 and calcium 41 in the Shroud, that would indicate that there was a nuclear disintegration and a low temperature nuclear reaction.[194]

If that were the case and we know how the image was produced, then we'd also know that carbon dating will never work under any circumstances on this material because when you have neutron flux, it will change N14 into C14, and C14 is what you look for in a carbon-14 dating. There will be an overabundance of carbon-14, skewing the results.[195]

The date of the Shroud remains uncertain. But there are credible objections to the dating methods of the 1988 team. If, as it seems likely, the image was produced by radiation, the main question left is this: How on earth does a human body spontaneously produce that much radiation?

Without the answer to that question, we won't find an answer to the mystery of the Shroud. Perhaps science doesn't hold all the answers. It could be that the light of history and faith will uncover what science can't.

8

A Story Told by Wounds

The Gospel accounts of the crucifixion and resurrection of Jesus offer an extraordinary level of detail that is consistent across the Gospels.[196] Biblical scholar Luke Timothy Johnson explains:

> The accounts of Jesus' last days—called passion narratives—reported in all four Gospels offer a partial exception to these general observations. In contrast to the episodic and loosely joined pericopes in the sections of the narratives dealing with Jesus' ministry, the passion accounts (starting with the Last Supper and extending through the burial) are remarkable for the way they present a lengthy, sequential, and connected story. Furthermore, they are notable for the attention they give to details, including the time and place that events occurred. Most remarkable is the relatively high degree of agreement among the four versions. Such agreement might be expected among the Synoptics. But in this case

> we find it also between the Synoptics and John. There is every reason to think that this part of the Jesus story reached some form of concrete and stable expression (whether oral or written) early on, and that its basic shape survived even the redactional work of the four evangelists.[197]

Many reputable scientists who have studied the Shroud believe that the image appears to be that of a victim of crucifixion. Pierre Barbet, a French physician, stated that the wounds were consistent with those typically suffered by a crucified man and are "almost perfect from an anatomical point of view." Columbia University's Frederick Zugibe agreed that the image was of a crucifixion victim.[198]

Specifically, the wounds seem to indicate that the man in the Shroud was Jesus of Nazareth.

For example, the man on the Shroud has obvious wounds on his face. The image shows a bruised face and possibly a broken nose. All four Gospels likewise report that Jesus was beaten across the face by the Romans.[199]

The biblical texts do not give many details on the method of torture that the guards inflicted on Jesus, but historical archaeological objects and texts can help us narrow down the circumstances of the historical flagellation. As Dr. Verschuuren explains:

> The instrument of scourging was the dreaded Roman scourging whip, or flagellum, the thongs of which had sharp pieces of metal or bone attached at a short distance from the tips. The Shroud of Turin reveals more than 120 scourging wounds over the victim's body, most notably on his back, which indicates that he was bound with his face to a column and his arms above his head.

> If each flagellum had only two thongs, he must have received at least sixty strokes. Two of the flogging guards, one standing on either side of the victim, applied these strokes alternately and mercilessly.[200]

At the time of Jesus' crucifixion, the Romans often used the flagrum, a whip with metal pellets fastened to the ends, to administer floggings. The tips were shaped like dumbbells so as to tear into the deep layers of flesh and inflict maximum pain. Jesus' body would have been bruised. His muscles would have hemorrhaged, and his lungs may have collapsed.[201]

It is highly unlikely that a medieval forger had ever seen a Roman flagrum or had even been aware of the specifications of such a weapon.

As if the whipping weren't sufficiently painful and humiliating, the Gospel accounts say that the Roman soldiers also fashioned a crown of thorns for Jesus, mocking him for claiming to be the King of the Jews. Three of the four Gospels — Matthew, Mark, and John — mention the crown of thorns.[202] This was not standard procedure for Roman crucifixions. It's probably safe to assume that the soldiers wanted to inflict the maximum amount of pain that they could. The way that Romans wove the crown was in the shape of a cap (rather than a circlet) to get the maximum number of thorns pressed down on the top of the head and to produce intense suffering.[203]

That is precisely what is portrayed the Shroud. It's as if somebody has taken a clump of thorns and thrusted it on top of the person's head. Blood stains are seen on the forehead and down the side of his face, suggesting that there were wounds or lacerations on the head. As Dr. Zugibe explains:

> The images corresponding to the forehead ... reveal a backward 3 impression on the left

> forehead position, a bifurcated stream on the right forehead, which continues into the hair, and several individual images on the brow and in the hair. Several tortuous streams are noted in the hair that extend to the base. This pattern is consistent with wounds created by the crown of thorns, which was plaited into a cap rather than into a circlet. . . .
>
> The number 3 configuration on the forehead has been postulated to be due to deep furrows of the forehead, but . . . the more practical explanation is that following the removal of the cap of thorns, dislodgment of the clots or dried blood would cause blood to ooze out of the puncture wounds. If the body was being carried to the tomb, the movements of the body would easily account for the tortuous flow.[204]

Blood pooled around the back of the head of the man in the Shroud. This is consistent with the trauma caused by the crown of thorns. This leads us to the question: Do corpses bleed? Dr. Zugibe continues:

> In sudden or violent deaths, such as severe trauma, automobile accidents, electrocutions, concussions, and gunshot blasts, clotting initially may begin, but in a matter of fifteen minutes or one-half hour, the blood becomes fluid again. This is not a firm rule; we frequently see fluid blood in individuals with severe disease and coagulated blood in individuals following sudden or violent deaths, but only on rare occasions in the latter case. . . .

> The answer to the question whether blood might flow after death in the case of Jesus may now be answered in the affirmative because his death fulfills the criteria of a violent death that could lead to fluidity of the blood.[205]

The additional face and head wounds, which are noted in the Gospels, would account for the amount of blood present on the Shroud.

The Gospels seem to indicate that the nail wounds were in Jesus' hands. In the Shroud image, it looks as if they are in the wrists. There are several theories about how Jesus was hung on the cross. Some posit that the nails were placed through his wrists, as studies have shown that the hand flesh is not substantial enough to support the weight of a fully grown man.

The only uncovered remains of Jewish victims of crucifixion show that the nails were likely anchored in the wrists.[206] If the nails went through the wrists, they would have pierced a central nerve in the arm, causing intense pain.

Similarly, nails were driven through either the feet or the ankles. Nails driven through the ankles would have hit another crucial nerve; the pain from the combination of severe damage to both nerves would cause violent full-body spasms.

Dr. Barbet conducted tests on cadavers to find the likeliest placement of the nails in crucifixion victims. He determined that there is a spot where the wrist bones would support the weight of a human on a cross without tearing through the flesh, as nails driven through the palms might do.[207]

Barbet argues:

> The wrist consists of two rows of four small bones, known as the carpal bones. These eight bones of the wrist are located in the heel of

> the hand, at the part of the palm closest to the forearm. This location would allow the nails to support the weight of an adult man because the ligaments that join the eight wrist bones are thicker and stronger than those that connect the bones of the palm (the metacarpal bones).[208]

Frederick Zugibe shows that the nails do not just pierce the wrists. He argues that they go right into the lower part of the palm at a 10-degree angle, pointing down through a cluster of nerves at a very sturdy part of the wrist. The protruding mark on the Shroud image is the exit wound in the back of the wrist.

Another point about the image in the Shroud is that the thumbs are not visible. But this is consistent with how the hands might be set together after the person has died. As Dr. Zugibe explains:

> The reason that the thumbs are not visible is common knowledge to anyone in forensic pathology. The deceased individuals transferred to our medical examiner's office from the local hospitals have their wrists crossed and tied together, and in every case the thumbs are in a position in front of and slightly to the side of the index fingers. This is a relatively natural postmortem position. It would be almost impossible to have impressions of the thumbs because the Shroud would not be in contact with them except perhaps for a slight segment at the base near the hand. The fingers appear long and clawlike. There are two explanations for this. The first is related to the compression by the nail in the thenar furrow, causing an extension

effect of the fingers; the second may be arachnodactyly (claw-hands) from Marfan's Syndrome.[209]

The image on the Shroud also shows that the man has a wound in his right side, between the fifth and sixth ribs.[210] There is blood under the wound that runs to his back. There is also a watery substance with the blood.

John's Gospel attests that a centurion pierced Jesus' side with a spear and blood and water flowed out of his side. (Roman soldiers were trained to aim at a potentially lethal spot below the armpit in the chest.[211]) As we discussed, this was done in lieu of breaking his legs — the Romans' more usual method of hastening the death of one who had been crucified.

Sure enough, the image on the Shroud corroborates the description John gives of the wound inflicted on Jesus by the soldier.[212] Additionally, the legs of the man depicted in the Shroud image are not broken.

It was only by seeing the wounds on Jesus' body that "Doubting Thomas" truly believed that Jesus had risen from the dead. Many today have found the same confirmation by gazing at the same wounds on the Shroud.

9

A Crucifixion and Resurrection?

We have come to the end of our investigation and the mystery of the missing body. We've examined the historical record, cross-examined the key witnesses, and consulted the lab reports.

So what occurred in the tomb? Where is the body?

Jesus says, "I am the light of the world; he who follows me will not walk in darkness, but will have the light of life."[213] Well, all the facts point back to the light as the culprit in our two-thousand-year-old cold case.

Considering the evidence, it appears that this light contributed to the creation of the image on the Shroud.

But what kind of light? And how did it leave a negative image on the Shroud? And finally, where is the body? Is it a coincidence that the only account that makes sense is the one told by the witnesses in the Bible — namely, that Jesus rose from the dead?

We have heard from chemists, radiologists, philosophers, and scholars, but there seems to be no better explanation than that found in the Bible. If biblical witnesses testify that Jesus rose from the dead, body and soul, this means that his claims to divinity were not blasphemy, as Caiaphas claimed. If Jesus was indeed resurrected, that means he might just be what he claimed to be in Holy Writ — the Son of God — and the Christian proclamation would be true.

In light of the evidence, let's re-examine the biblical account of Jesus' last days. What's the message found in his last days, in the crucifixion and the resurrection? What is this new and controversial message that Jesus introduced to the world?

What was his crime?

The fact is, Jesus was controversial, and that was not accidental. He said he did not come to bring peace on earth. In fact, the Gospel accounts record that he provoked quite the opposite effect. He created division in the Jewish ranks. Some among the Jewish elite, such as Caiaphas, facilitated his death, whereas others, such as Joseph of Arimathea and Nicodemus, tended to his burial.

This wasn't a coincidence, either. Jesus drew the battle lines and openly confessed that he brought "a sword."[214] He was open about his rejection of authority, even the Jewish authorities:

> Then said Jesus to the crowds and to his disciples, "The scribes and the Pharisees sit on Moses' seat; so practice and observe whatever they tell you, but not what they do; for they preach, but do not practice. They bind heavy burdens, hard to bear, and lay them on men's shoulders; but they themselves will not move them with their finger. . . .
>
> "He who is greatest among you shall be your servant; whoever exalts himself will be humbled, and whoever humbles himself will be exalted."[215]

Jesus told his followers to face persecution by turning the other cheek. Some viewed this as submissive and pacifistic. Others saw it as a rebellion against authority — a way of encouraging his followers to stand their ground if they were wronged by those in power.[216]

Jesus also preached about helping the poorest and the weakest in society. The only recorded instance in which Jesus was violent was when he turned over the tables of the money changers in the Temple:

> Jesus entered the temple of God and drove out all who sold and bought in the temple, and he overturned the tables of the money-changers and the seats of those who sold pigeons. He said to them, "It is written, 'My house shall be called a house of prayer'; but you make it a den of robbers."[217]

It was an attempt to purify the Temple from Roman coinage.[218]

Jesus stood up to the authorities to preach the truth, that he was the way and the light, even to the point of being put to death on a cross. Caiaphas asked if Jesus was the Son of God. Jesus responded: "You have said so." What's more, he warned his accusers that they would "see the Son of man seated at the right hand of Power, and coming on the clouds of Heaven."

Caiaphas rent his garments. He had heard the blasphemy from Jesus' own lips.[219] Jesus was now a criminal in Caiaphas's eyes — a criminal who deserved death.

But if they wanted Jesus dead, they needed a different kind of evidence. The Romans didn't care if he was a wayward Jew. They cared only about upholding the Pax Romana. So, the Jewish leaders had to show that Jesus was a threat to the civil order as well.

Whether they knew it or not, their own king had feared Jesus for just that reason — only, back then, Jesus was just a baby:

> Now when Jesus was born in Bethlehem of Judea in the days of Herod the king, behold, wise men

> from the East came to Jerusalem, saying, "Where is he who has been born king of the Jews? For we have seen his star in the East, and have come to worship him." When Herod the king heard this, he was troubled, and all Jerusalem with him; and assembling all the chief priests and scribes of the people, he inquired of them where the Christ was to be born.[220]

The point is, political leaders did not take claims to royalty lightly. So Caiaphas and his followers informed the Romans that Jesus called himself King of the Jews. He was making himself a rival to Caesar! The Romans had to execute him.[221] They had no choice.

Or so Caiaphas said.

The Roman governor, Pilate, went along with the high priest and commanded that a sign that read "Jesus of Nazareth, King of the Jews" be hung on Jesus' cross. Caiaphas protested. The chief priests protested. "Do not write, 'The King of the Jews,' but, 'This man said, I am King of the Jews', they insisted." But Pilate was adamant. "What I have written I have written."[222]

Jesus was marched to Golgotha after being whipped and beaten, not only by the Romans but also by the Jewish police. His head was bleeding because of the crown of the thorns that had been mockingly bestowed by the Roman guards who administered his torture.

They placed the cross on Jesus' shoulders and then began the march to Golgotha. Jesus was exhausted. He stumbled under the weight of the cross. It knocked against his shoulder and made him fall and bruise his knees . Simon of Cyrene took up the cross for a while.

The image of the man on the Shroud corroborates the historicity of these moments when Jesus was wounded during his passion. The image shows wounds from the torture that the Roman guards inflicted, the right shoulder appears to be dislocated or have abrasions on the skin,[223] and the legs are bruised.

The Gospels say Jesus died relatively quickly once he was crucified. He was pierced in the side by a centurion. In his Gospel, John claims he has eyewitness testimony to prove that this happened:

> Since it was the day of Preparation, in order to prevent the bodies from remaining on the cross on the sabbath (for that sabbath was a high day), the Jews asked Pilate that their legs might be broken, and that they might be taken away. So the soldiers came and broke the legs of the first, and of the other who had been crucified with him; but when they came to Jesus and saw that he was already dead, they did not break his legs. But one of the soldiers pierced his side with a spear, and at once there came out blood and water. He who saw it has borne witness—his testimony is true, and he knows that he tells the truth—that you also may believe.[224]

Jesus was hurriedly taken down from the cross so that his disciples could keep the Sabbath. The Gospel of Matthew says that Jesus was placed in a new tomb that Joseph of Arimathea had hewn out of rock for his own burial. Here perhaps is the first mention of the Shroud:

> When it was evening, there came a rich man from Arimathea, named Joseph, who also was a disciple of Jesus. He went to Pilate and asked for the body of Jesus. Then Pilate ordered it to be given to him. And Joseph took the body, and wrapped it in a clean linen shroud, and laid it

> in his own new tomb, which he had hewn in the rock; and he rolled a great stone to the door of the tomb, and departed.[225]

The Gospel of Mark also mentions Jesus' burial shroud:

> And Pilate wondered if he were already dead; and summoning the centurion, he asked him whether he was already dead. And when he learned from the centurion that he was dead, he granted the body to Joseph. And he bought a linen shroud, and taking him down, wrapped him in the linen shroud, and laid him in a tomb which had been hewn out of the rock; and he rolled a stone against the door of the tomb. Mary Magdalene and Mary the mother of Jesus saw where he was laid.[226]

Luke 23:53 contains yet another mention of the burial Shroud of Christ: "Then he took it down and wrapped it in a linen shroud, and laid him in a rock-hewn tomb, where no one had ever yet been laid." So does John 19:39–40: "Nicodemus also, who had at first come to him by night, came bringing a mixture of myrrh and aloes, about a hundred pounds' weight. They took the body of Jesus, and bound it in linen cloths with the spices, as is the burial custom of the Jews."

In Rome, the bodies of the crucified were left on the crosses to rot. But in Israel, for the purity of the land, no one would ever be left hanging from a tree or a cross. The body would be properly buried.

In fact, Jewish law required the Sanhedrin to see to the burial of anybody they condemned to death. Joseph and Nicodemus believed in Jesus' message, so they arranged a proper burial for him. Joseph of Arimathea took Jesus' body down and put it in a tomb that had never been used.

Only the elite could afford tombs such as these, which were covered by a rolling stone. Jesus was being treated not as a criminal who had conspired against the state but as a man of great dignity, even royalty — which contrasted sharply with the shameful manner of his death.

As a wealthy member of the elite Jewish ruling class, Joseph of Arimathea could afford all the accoutrements of a properly executed Jewish burial, linens included.

Part of the reason the stone was so important was that grave robbing was ubiquitous in the ancient Near Eastern World. Archaeologists have discovered an ancient tablet with a proclamation from Caesar prohibiting grave robbing. Some say it is from Nazareth, but its origins are hotly disputed.[227]

Normally, the authorities feared that grave robbers would take the valuable items left in the tomb. In Jesus' case, however, the Jewish authorities feared that his disciples would come and steal his body and spread rumors of a resurrection. Once he was dead and buried, his movement would fizzle out. Cut off the head, and the body would die. Then their troubles would be over.

Rome also had a vested interest in protecting the tomb. The political authorities would not want a criminal, an enemy of the state, to be publicly revered, so they would likely lend their guards willingly. Criminals were not to be honored or publicly lamented.[228]

Despite all the precautions taken by the Jewish authorities and the Roman guard to prevent word of a risen Jesus, by Sunday morning, the body was gone. Mary Magdalene, the first witness, reported this to the disciples. They came to see for themselves. Just as Mary said, the body was gone; only the linens were left behind:

> Now on the first day of the week Mary Magdalene came to the tomb early, while it was still dark, and saw that the stone had been taken away from

> the tomb. So she ran, and went to Simon Peter and the other disciple, the one whom Jesus loved, and said to them, "They have taken the Lord out of the tomb, and we do not know where they have laid him." Peter then came out with the other disciple, and they went toward the tomb. They both ran, but the other disciple outran Peter and reached the tomb first; and stooping to look in, he saw the linen cloths lying there, but he did not go in. Then Simon Peter came, following him, and went into the tomb; he saw the linen cloths lying, and the napkin, which had been on his head, not lying with the linen cloths but rolled up in a place by itself. Then the other disciple, who reached the tomb first, also went in, and he saw and believed; for as yet they did not know the scripture, that he must rise from the dead.[229]

The disciples were in awe of what had happened. They, like the Pharisees, wondered where the body was. The Gospels report that Jesus appeared to Mary and the disciples in his risen state, with the wounds he sustained from the passion:

> On the evening of that day, the first day of the week, the doors being shut where the disciples were, for fear of the Jews, Jesus came and stood among them and said to them, "Peace be with you." When he had said this, he showed them his hands and his side. Then the disciples were glad when they saw the Lord. Jesus said to them again, "Peace be with you. As the Father has sent me, even so I send you." And when he

> had said this, he breathed on them, and said to them, "Receive the Holy Spirit. If you forgive the sins of any, they are forgiven; if you retain the sins of any, they are retained."[230]

The Gospel accounts of the resurrected Jesus signify that Jesus' body was transformed. In 1 Corinthians 15:44, St. Paul calls it a *soma pneumatikon*, a natural body energized by the Spirit of God.[231] There was no such concept in Judaism. This was one of Jesus' most radical new teachings.[232]

Mary Magdalene, the first to see the resurrected Jesus, did not even recognize her friend:

> But Mary stood weeping outside the tomb, and as she wept she stooped to look into the tomb; and she saw two angels in white, sitting where the body of Jesus had lain, one at the head and one at the feet. They said to her, "Woman, why are you weeping?" She said to them, "Because they have taken away my Lord, and I do not know where they have laid him." Saying this, she turned round and saw Jesus standing, but she did not know that it was Jesus. Jesus said to her, "Woman, why are you weeping? Whom do you seek?" Supposing him to be the gardener, she said to him, "Sir, if you have carried him away, tell me where you have laid him, and I will take him away." Jesus said to her, "Mary." She turned and said to him in Hebrew, "Rabboni!" (which means Teacher). Jesus said to her, "Do not hold me, for I have not yet ascended to the Father; but go to my brethren and say to them, I am ascending

> to my Father and your Father, to my God and your God." Mary Magdalene went and said to the disciples, "I have seen the Lord"; and she told them that he had said these things to her.[233]

Parallels of the resurrection can be seen in the transfiguration of Christ (which points to the resurrection), when, in the case of the transfiguration, he was bathed in light. This shocked the three apostles who were at the transfiguration, Peter, James, and John. Matthew's Gospel says that when Jesus appeared transfigured on the mountain, they all bowed down in worship. The transfiguration was so complete that Jesus still had to identify himself to his friends before they recognized him.

When Jesus appears to Mary, as reported in John's Gospel, why do the guards not recognize him as the man from the tomb? Could his physical transformation be the reason? Perhaps elements of metaphysical nature transformed his body and obscured their human senses.

How does that happen? Jesus claims that it was through the power of his Father, God. And the same power was manifested at the resurrection.

Still, the Gospel of Luke says Jesus' followers suspected that Jesus was a ghost — maybe because he entered the room without using the door! Their first reaction to his reappearance was terror. In fact, three Greek verbs meaning "terrify" are used by Luke. Still, in short order, they came to believe that Jesus had indeed risen from the dead.

Thomas was not there when Jesus first appeared and said, "Unless I see in his hands the print of the nails, and place my finger in the mark of the nails, and place my hand in his side, I will not believe." So, Jesus came back again. Thomas saw the wounds on Jesus' palms and side and confessed, "My Lord and my God!"[234]

Thomas wasn't swearing. He meant, "The Lord of me; the God of me." He was saying that Jesus is the Lord. He is God. In this way, he is the light.

10

CRIME SCENE DO NOT CROS

Face-to-Face

The death of Jesus was the most consequential death in human history. In some, Jesus inspires worship and adoration. For others, he represents a challenge to their way of life.

Consider Jesus' encounter with the rich man:

> Behold, one came up to him, saying, "Teacher, what good deed must I do, to have eternal life?" And he said to him, "Why do you ask me about what is good? One there is who is good. If you would enter life, keep the commandments." He said to him, "Which?" And Jesus said, "You shall not kill, You shall not commit adultery, You shall not steal, You shall not bear false witness, Honor your father and mother, and, You shall love your neighbor as yourself." The young man said to him, "All these I have observed; what do I still lack?" Jesus said to him, "If you would be perfect, go, sell what you possess and give to the poor, and you will have treasure in

> heaven; and come, follow me." When the young man heard this he went away sorrowful; for he had great possessions.[235]

The Bible isn't simply a collection of fairy tales, nor is it a scientific or purely historical document. For believers it's divine revelation. As such, it is also in many ways a manual for life, a sinner's guide to the galaxy. It speaks to the fallen nature of the human condition.

Many of the leading figures in the Bible are historical, but at the same time they embody different sins and personalities. We can learn invaluable life lessons from the failures and sins of biblical figures.

Pontius Pilate was a relativist. Although he didn't believe in Jesus' guilt, he still allowed him to be crucified because it was the popular wish of the crowd. Caiaphas was egotistical and power hungry. Mary Magdalene was a reformed sinner. Peter was a strong, albeit flawed, leader.

We can find people like these everywhere in the world today. Our flaws are reflected in the biblical figures. There are still Caiaphases and Pilates, but there are also Marys, Peters, and Johns.

Likewise, a similar spectrum of opinions on Jesus and his message in the first century is still represented in society. Jesus is still as scandalous and controversial as he was in the first century. Some fear to look at him face-to-face because he challenges our basic human instincts and human vanities.

Just as there were personal motives behind his crucifixion in the first century, so in the heart of modern man, there are ulterior motives not to believe in him. It's not that science is incompatible with faith. Modern science was born not of doubt but of faith. It wasn't that scientists became disillusioned with the God of Genesis and wanted to discover how the universe really works. No: they believed in the God of Genesis and wanted to understand how he works.

Nicolaus Copernicus, the astronomer and mathematician who revolutionized science by proposing that Earth orbits the Sun, not the other way around, was one of the foremost scientific thinkers who saw the nexus between faith and science. He said:

> To know the mighty works of God; to comprehend His wisdom and majesty and power; to appreciate, in degree, the wonderful working of His Laws, surely all this must be a pleasing and acceptable mode of worship to the Most High, to whom ignorance cannot be more grateful than knowledge.

During the Renaissance, a chasm between religion and science began to grow. By the Enlightenment and nineteenth century, the rift seemed unbridgeable to many thinkers, including Karl Marx, Auguste Comte, and Ludwig Feuerbach. Science focused strictly on empirical studies — what we can see, smell, touch, or taste — and shoved the metaphysical aside. As Fr. Andrew Dalton argues, scientism replaced science.[236] Faith and reason were seen as mutually exclusive.

Even the Bible recognizes that faith and natural reason are not contradictory but are innately intertwined.[237] Paul explains the connection in Romans 1:19–20: "For what can be known about God is plain to them, because God has shown it to them. Ever since the creation of the world his invisible nature, namely, his eternal power and deity, has been clearly perceived in the things that have been made."

As if in reaction to the positivism of the 1800s, the turn of the twentieth century saw the advent of new scientific techniques revive the somewhat dormant scientific aspect of Christianity. A photo of the Shroud of Turin breathed a new hopeful spirit of faith into the public square.

Could Christianity as defined by the modern world once again become the transformative message of the West?

In our investigation of whether the Shroud of Turin is the burial cloth of Jesus, we have moved the bar from plausibility to probability, even to high probability. If one considers the history, art, and science as supporting sources outside of the Bible, the evidence is in favor of the theory that it is the genuine burial cloth of Christ.

As science advances, what was once widely considered a phony holy relic is now looking more legitimate than ever. As Max Planck, the physicist who invented quantum theory, famously stated, "Science progresses funeral by funeral."

As we peer into the face of the Shroud, we can still hear the man in the Shroud asking: "Who do you say I am?"

Caiaphas had an answer, as did Peter, Paul, and Pontius Pilate. How they answered the question would significantly impact their lives. Was he the Messiah? A King? And if so, what kind of king?

Jesus said, "My kingship is not of this world; if my kingship were of this world, my servants would fight, that I might not be handed over to the Jews; but my kingship is not from the world."[238]

His dominion does, however, extend to Earth. Although he rules a heavenly kingdom, it is made manifest on Earth. Jesus was saying that he is a king, but he's not like other earthly kings. He's the King of Heaven who also rules on Earth.

Rebelling against that law might be the very instinct embedded in us with the advent of original sin. That is why the ideas of disobedience and pure autonomy are connected with the ability to attain knowledge and wisdom.[239]

"Then Jesus told his disciples, 'If any man would come after me, let him deny himself and take up his cross and follow me. For whoever would save his life will lose it, and whoever loses his life for my sake will find it.' "[240]

Obedience means death. And yet the King commands us to take up our crosses every day and follow him. In a way, his crucifixion and willing death scramble our investigation by removing the human motive — motives to gain, kill, or neglect. Jesus told his followers that he would lay down his life for them.

If the story is true, Jesus dies because of a promise, and ultimately, he rises because of that promise in a covenant of redemption. He says he will come again to fulfill his covenant and bring about the ultimate redemption of this world in a second coming. Living in a world filled with suffering and evil, many might distrust promises of a happily ever after.

After thoroughly investigating the case's facts, we can conclude that the Shroud of Turin is very likely the burial cloth of Jesus of Nazareth. It contains everything we would expect such a cloth to contain and more. Now it's the skeptics who bear the burden of proof, not the believers.

John A. T. Robinson, the former dean of chapel at Trinity College in Cambridge and a skeptic turned believer, argued that while there may not be hard proof yet of the Shroud's authenticity, the odds are undeniably in its favor.

> For myself I would assume that we are here neither in the world of sheer unaccountable miracle nor in that of repeatable experiment but in that mysterious realm of paranormal physical phenomena which appear to accompany intense mystical and spiritual states. All one can do is to press on into the unknown with what partial parallels one can find, retaining both the openness and the skepticism which has marked psychical research at its best.[241]

While the world of skepticism has hidden behind a wall of science, the Shroud opens a crack and allows new light to break through — a light that says there is more to life than this. Although we do not have all the answers to what happened on that Sunday two thousand years ago, perhaps some mysteries are best left for after death, when we are ready to meet Jesus face-to-face.

Epilogue

For two thousand years, the death of a carpenter has remained shrouded in mystery.

There's no trace of the body of the man who inspired sacrifice yet sparked hatred. His execution came swiftly because he challenged the authority of the preeminent political and religious leaders of his nation.

He forced those in power to confront his revolutionary doctrine and claims to a coming kingdom. The powers that be guarded his tomb so that no one could claim that he rose from the dead, as he said he would.

Alas, it was all in vain: the body was gone two days later. Only the Shroud remained.

Even today, the faded image of his bloodied face and his open wounds, kept safe in the city of Turin, Italy, inspires millions of people from all walks of life to embrace his dying wish: "Forgive them."[242]

Neither chemist nor physicist nor scholar can totally explain the mystery behind how the image of this man's face came to be on this ancient linen sheet.

Like his Shroud, Jesus' story has lived on beyond his era. His revolutionary message has transcended time and has been passed down the ages to the present day.

His disciples claimed that Jesus was the Son of the living God—that he had risen.

Who do you say he is?

Acknowledgments

The inspiration for this book began with the loss of my father and was sustained by an introduction to some special people with a great passion for the Shroud. Though I started as a skeptic, my straightforward investigation became a journey blending the worlds of science and faith and ending with a special encounter.

Writing a book from the perspective of my own journey has been an internal and, at times, interactive process. For that reason, I will forever be indebted to Fr. Andrew Dalton for his vast knowledge, keen insights, and ongoing support. I also want to thank Ila Stanger and Erin McLaughlin for their feedback and editorial help. Because of their efforts and encouragement, I can now tell this story in full.

A special thanks goes out to Jason Pearson, a partner and a pillar of support, along with the Shroud Center of Southern California Team: August Accetta, M.D., Lee Sweeney, Nora Creech, Deacon Peter Lauder, Deacon Gary Griffin, Ralph Linzmeier, Mark McElrath, Dan Dulac, Lisa Rowan, Dave Belz, and Michael Manhardt. I must also thank the team's generous donors: David Andrade, Jason Neff, Shirley Varsel, Phillip Ramos, William Marquart, Keith Myers, Sharon E. Videtich, Susan Mary Strader, David Alan Lawrence,

Pablo E. Moysam Davila, Thomas Grebel, Diane Rinella, David Klein, Rita Russo, P. J. Kosten, Susan Biffle, Richard French, April Mahfood, Gordon Ferrell, Angel Gonzalez, Eric Anderson, and David Sumida.

I am grateful to the scholars who sat through my interrogations in the interview seat, including Fr. Spitzer, Dale Allison, Mark Goodacre, Ben Witherington, Emanuela Marinelli, and Fr. Dalton — though there were many more. And I thank everyone on the Sophia Institute team for all their support and efforts to help me turn my ideas into a book.

As always, I thank my wife, Margo, whom I was always able to turn to during dark times, and my son, Dante, who is beginning to take his own journey. I am also grateful for having been reminded how suffering can lead to deep gratitude and even greater revelation.

Appendix 1

Timeline of the Shroud

Circa AD 30/33

Jesus is crucified, buried, and resurrected.

The apostle Thaddeus brings King Abgar of Edessa a cloth with Jesus' resemblance on it, and the king is reported to have been healed of leprosy by the cloth, which becomes known as the Image of Edessa, or the Mandylion.

AD 66–70

The siege of Jerusalem forces many Jews to flee the city, after which the Shroud may have been moved out of Jerusalem to safety in Antioch.

Circa AD 66–110

The Gospels of Matthew, Mark, Luke, and John are written. They give eyewitness accounts of the burial shroud of Jesus.

AD 544

Legend has it that a cloth "not by hand made" and "doubled in four" is found hidden in the wall of the city of Edessa after the siege of the Persians.

Around the late fourth century, artistic depictions of Jesus start to have a beard and generally resemble the image on the Shroud.

Circa AD 943–944

The Byzantine emperor buys the Image of Edessa from the Arabs in control of Edessa, and the image is transported from Edessa to Constantinople.

Circa 1050

Artists depict the Image of Edessa in their art.

1130

There are now recorded accounts of the Shroud with "the form and size of the Lord's body."

Circa 1192

The Hungarian minister sketches a body of Jesus that resembles the Shroud, including the burn marks on the linen.

Circa 1204

Crusader Robert de Clari claims he saw "the shroud in which our Lord had been wrapped" in Constantinople. The Shroud disappears in the Sack of Constantinople.

1205

A controversial letter to the pope claims that the Shroud had been moved to Athens and is being kept by Otho de la Roche.

1357

Public displays of the Shroud are held in a chapel in Lirey by the wife of Geoffrey de Charny.

1389

Bishop Pierre d'Arcis writes to Pope Clement VII that the Shroud is an artist's forgery.

1453

The Shroud is transferred from the Charnys to the Savoys.

1502

The Shroud is housed in a chapel in Chambéry.

1532

A fire in the Chambéry chapel partially damages the Shroud, but the image is left intact.

1535

The Shroud is shuttled around France as invaders enter.

1561

The Shroud returns to Chambéry.

1578

The Shroud moves to Turin, where it will largely stay until the present.

1694

The Shroud is placed in the completed Shroud chapel.

1898

The Shroud is photographed by Secondo Pia during a public showing of the Shroud, accidentally revealing in the negative a surprisingly detailed image of a crucified man.

1931

Photographer Giuseppe Enrie takes more black and white photos of the Shroud, which testify to the veracity of Pia's photos.

1978

The Shroud of Turin Research Project (STURP) commences its scientific analysis of the Shroud.

1979

STURP announces that the Shroud is not an artist's forgery.

1983

The Shroud becomes the property of the Vatican.

1988

Carbon-14 dating tests date the Shroud back to the Middle Ages.

1997

The Shroud is almost destroyed by another fire.

2002

The Shroud Conservation Project begins. The first full scans of the Shroud are taken.

2017

The British Museum releases raw data from the carbon-14 dating experiments, leading researchers to question the accuracy of the results and the age of the Shroud.[243]

2018

The first 3D model of the man in the Shroud is created.

Appendix 2

Key Witnesses

Caiaphas: Appointed by the governor preceding Pilate, Caiaphas was the high priest of the Jewish Temple from AD 18 to 37. His father-in-law, Annas, was the high priest before him. Caiaphas ordered the arrest of Jesus at Gethsemane and sent him to the Roman governor, Pontius Pilate, to be crucified. He saw Jesus and his large following as a threat to his power and the traditions of the Jewish religion.

Herod Antipas: Tetrarch of Galilee. Pontius Pilate sent Jesus to Herod when he learned that Jesus was a Galilean and under Herod's purview. Pilate consulted with Herod on whether to crucify Jesus. Herod reportedly did not see Jesus as a threat and returned him to Pilate.[244]

Pontius Pilate: Governor of Judea from AD 26 to 36 under the Roman emperor Tiberius Caesar. Views of Pilate vary wildly among historians. Some see Pilate as one of Judea's harshest governors; others think he was too lenient. Pilate was in Jerusalem to keep the peace during the typically raucous Jewish Passover when the Jewish authorities handed Jesus over to him to be judged for crucifixion. According to several sources, Pilate did not find Jesus guilty of a crime against the state, but fearing that the crowd might riot, he sentenced Jesus to death by crucifixion.

John: Son of Zebedee and brother of the apostle James; also known as St. John the Evangelist and the "disciple whom Jesus loved." John was one of Jesus' inner circle of three apostles and a leader of the early church. He wrote several books in the biblical canon: one of the four Gospels, the three letters of John, and the book of Revelation. He was at the Last Supper and was likely there when the Jewish authorities arrested Jesus and interrogated him before handing him over to Pontius Pilate. Subsequently he was the only disciple present at the crucifixion. He gave a very detailed account of Jesus' last days and wrote about seeing Jesus' empty tomb, including the burial cloths.

James: Brother of the apostle John. Not to be confused with James, Son of Alphaeus, another one of the Twelve. James was in Jesus' inner circle, along with Peter and John, and was at the Last Supper and in the Garden of Gethsemane.

James, the brother of Jesus: The Catholic and Eastern Orthodox traditions hold that John was a cousin of Jesus, rather than a brother or stepbrother, but also see Jewish and Islamic thinkers.[245]

Mary, the mother of Jesus: Daughter of Anne and Joachim. She was married to Joseph around age fourteen. She was the cousin of Elizabeth, the mother of John the Baptist. Mary was at the crucifixion of her son. She is venerated in many Christian churches as the Virgin Mother of God.

Mary Magdalene: A woman of ill repute whom Jesus reformed. She became a close follower of Jesus, was present at the crucifixion, and was also witness when Jesus appeared to her after his death.

Mark: Author of the Gospel of Mark. He was a contemporary of Jesus but was not one of the Twelve. He was rumored to be close to the apostle Peter.

Peter: One of the Twelve, whom Jesus called "rock" and instituted as the leader of his church. Peter was present at the Last Supper, in the

Garden of Gethsemane, and outside as Jesus was interrogated by the high priest, Caiaphas. Peter saw Jesus' tomb after the women informed him and the other apostles that the tomb was empty. He is reported to have seen the burial cloths of Christ in the tomb.

Matthew: One of the Twelve. He was a tax collector before he became a disciple of Jesus. He likely wrote the Gospel of Matthew.

Judas: One of the Twelve. After the Last Supper, he handed Jesus over to the chief priests for thirty pieces of silver.

Joseph of Arimathea: A wealthy member of the Sanhedrin and described as "good and righteous" in Luke's Gospel. Joseph buried Jesus in a large, expensive tomb. He is reported to have wrapped Jesus in burial cloths.

Nicodemus: An elite in Jewish society, Nicodemus was a well-respected Pharisee and a rich man. He met with Jesus and became his follower. When the Sanhedrin made plans against Jesus, Nicodemus spoke up on his behalf.[246] He also helped Joseph of Arimathea bury Jesus.

Paul: The apostle Paul was not one of the Twelve. He was a former Pharisee in charge of the Jewish police force that persecuted Christians. He claimed he had a vision of the risen Jesus and converted to Christianity. Paul is credited by some scholars with writing fourteen of the New Testament books in which he included testimony he received from Jesus' family members, including his brother James, and other eyewitness testimonies of Jesus' life.

Sanhedrin: The judicial body of the Jewish government, consisting in part of elders and chief priests. Three of the four Gospels claim that the Sanhedrin interrogated Jesus after his arrest by the Jewish authorities in the Garden of Gethsemane.

Sadducees: The Sadducees were leading Jewish priests who held political power. Although both the Sadducees and the Pharisees opposed

Jesus and his teachings, the two sects often clashed on doctrinal differences and struggled to maintain power. The Sadducees did not believe in the resurrection of the dead.

Centurions: Regarded by Julius Caesar as the backbone of the Roman forces, centurions were well-trained middle-ranking Roman officers, also found in the auxiliary regiments supplementing the legions.[247] They were either promoted from the ranks or transferred from a legion, and they might be Roman citizens (often recently enfranchised) or noncitizens. One of the Roman centurions speared Jesus' side on the cross to make sure he was dead. Notably, Jesus had cured the servant of one of the Roman centurions.

King Abgar V: The early Church historian Eusebius wrote about a Church tradition in which King Abgar V of Edessa supposedly received the Image of Edessa, what some people believe to be the burial cloth of Christ (or the Shroud of Turin). According to this tradition, Abgar was afflicted with leprosy and, having heard of Jesus' miraculous healings, wrote to him to implore him to come to Edessa to heal him. Jesus responded but did not go to Edessa. Instead, he sent his disciple Thaddeus. Not long after the resurrection, Thaddeus went to Edessa bearing a cloth with Jesus' likeness on it, and Abgar was miraculously healed.

Tacitus (ca. AD 56–ca. 120): Roman historian who documented that Jesus was crucified by Pontius Pilate.

Flavius Josephus (ca. AD 37–ca. 100): Jewish historian who documented that the Romans crucified Jesus.

Suetonius (ca. AD 69–ca. 122): Roman historian who wrote about Jesus, crediting him with founding the church.

Pliny the Younger (AD 62–113): Governor in Bithynia who wrote about the practices and beliefs of the early church.

Bibliography

Akyol, Mustafa. *The Islamic Jesus: How the King of the Jews Became a Prophet of the Muslims*. New York: St. Martin's Press, 2017.

Allen, David L. *Lukan Authorship of Hebrews*. Nashville: B&H Publishing Group, 2010.

Allison, Dale C., Jr. *Resurrecting Jesus: The Earliest Christian Tradition and Its Interpreters*. New York: T & T Clark International, 2005.

———. *The Resurrection of Jesus: Apologetics, Polemics, History*. London: Bloomsbury Publishing, 2021.

Allison, D. C., and W. D. Davies. *Matthew 8–18, International Critical Commentary*. Vol. 2. London: T&T Clark International, 2006.

Annet, Peter. *The Resurrection of Jesus in Answer to the Tryal of the Witnesses*. London: M. Cooper, 1744.

Aquinas, Thomas. *Compendium of Theology*. Translated by Cyril Vollert. Saint Louis: B. Herder, 1947.

Antonacci, M. "Particle Radiation from the Body Could Explain the Shroud's Images and Its Carbon Dating." *Scientific Research and Essays* 7, no. 29 (July 12, 2012): 2613–2623. Academic Journals. https://academicjournals.org/article/article1380798649_Antonacci.pdf.

Antonacci, Mark. *Resurrection of the Shroud: New Scientific, Medical, and Archaeological Evidence*. New York: M. Evans, 2000.

Associated Press. "Turin Shroud '3,000 Years Old,'" *Guardian*, January 29, 2005. https://www.theguardian.com/world/2005/jan/29/religion.uk.

Barbet, Pierre. *A Doctor at Calvary: The Passion of Our Lord Jesus Christ as Described by a Surgeon*. Garden City, NY: Image Books, 1963.

Barillas, Martin M. "Scientists Debunk Theory That Shroud of Turin Is Medieval Hoax." LifeSiteNews, July 24, 2019. https://www.lifesitenews.com/news/scientists-debunk-theory-that-shroud-of-turin-is-medieval-hoax/.

Barta, César. "The Shroud Sent to Louis IX of France by Baldwin II, the Latin Emperor at Constantople." Shroud of Turin website. https://www.shroud.com/pdfs/n56part5.pdf.

Beker, J. Christiaan. *Paul the Apostle: The Triumph of God in Life and Thought*. Philadelphia: Fortress Press, 1980.

Brown, Raymond E. *A Crucified Christ in Holy Week*. Collegeville, MN: Liturgical Press, 1986.

———. *An Introduction to the New Testament*. New York: Doubleday, 1997.

Raymond E. Brown, *The Death of the Messiah: From Gethsemane to the Grave*, Volume II, London: Geoffrey Chapman, 1994.

Burger, John. "New Data Questions Finding That Shroud of Turin Was a Medieval Hoax." Aleteia, July, 22, 2019. https://aleteia.org/2019/07/22/new-data-questions-finding-that-shroud-of-turin-was-medieval-hoax/.

Casabianca, T., E. Marinelli, G. Pernagallo, and B. Torrisi. "Radiocarbon Dating of the Turin Shroud: New Evidence from Raw Data" *Archaeometry* 65, no. 5 (March 22, 2019). https://philarchive.org/archive/CASTRD-3.

Casabianca, Tristan. "The Shroud of Turin: A Historiographical Approach." *Heythrop Journal* 54 (2013): 414–423.

Catholic News Agency. "Researcher Questions Whether Shroud Was Present at Last Supper." Catholic News Agency, April 27, 2006. https://www.catholicnewsagency.com/news/6595/researcher-questions-whether-shroud-was-present-at-last-supper.

Chinellato, Nicola. "Analyzing the Face on the Shroud of Turin with a Three-Dimensional Morphable Model." MA thesis, Utrecht University, 2017.

Ciskanik, Maggie. "5 Key Pieces of Evidence on the Shroud of Turin." Magis Center, August 7, 2018. https://www.magiscenter.com/blog/5-key-pieces-of-evidence-on-the-shroud-of-turin.

Cole, John R. Comments on "The Authentication of the Turin Shroud: An Issue in Archaeological Epistemology." *Current Anthropology* 24, no. 3 (1983): 296.

Crispino, Dorothy. "The Report of the Poor Clare Nuns: Chambéry, 1534." Shroud of Turin website. https://www.shroud.com/pdfs/ssi02part6.pdf.

Dalton, Andrew. "Shroud of Turin Retreat — Fr. Andrew Dalton, LC, Talk 1." YouTube video, 56:59. Posted by Real Faith Talks, March 26, 2019. https://www.youtube.com/watch?v=XcaPY2LsfKQ.

Danin, Avinoam. "Pressed Flowers: Where Did the Shroud of Turin Originate? A Botanical Quest." *Eretz* (November–December 1997). Shroud of Turin website. https://www.shroud.com/danin.htm.

Danto-Collins, Stephen. *Legions of Rome : The Definitive History of Every Imperial Roman Legion*. New York: St. Martin's Press, 2010.

Dostoevsky, Fyodor. *The Brothers Karamozov*. New York: Bantam Books, 1970.

Ehrman, Bart D. "Are the Gospels Historically Reliable? The Problem of Contradictions." YouTube video, 59:18, June 27, 2020. https://www.youtube.com/watch?v=AymnA526j9U.

———. "Did Jesus Exist?" *HuffPost,* May 20, 2012. https://www.huffpost.com/entry/did-jesus-exist_b_1349544.

———. *Did Jesus Exist? The Historical Argument for Jesus of Nazareth.* New York: Harper One, 2012.

———. "The Greek Manuscripts of the New Testament." *The Bart Ehrman Blog,* October 29, 2022. https://ehrmanblog.org/the-greek-manuscripts-of-the-new-testament/?utm_source=rss&utm_medium=rss&utm_campaign=the-greek-manuscripts-of-the-new-testament.

———. *Peter, Paul, and Mary Magdalene: The Followers of Jesus in History and Legend.* New York: Oxford University Press, 2006.

Evans, Craig, ed. *The Historical Jesus: Critical Concepts in Religious Studies.* Vol. 1. London: Routledge, 2004.

Evans, Craig A. *Jesus and His World: The Archaeological Evidence.* Louisville, KY: Westminster John Knox Press, 2012.

Evans, Craig A., and Tom Wright. *Jesus: The Final Days.* Edited by Troy A. Miller. London: Society for Promoting Christian Knowledge, 2008.

EWTN. "The Mystery of the Shroud of Turin." *EWTN News Nightly.*October 11, 2021, https://www.youtube.com/watch?v=MTmO_9Xy0E0.

Flury-Lemberg, Mechthild. "The Invisible Mending of Shroud in Theory and Reality." *British Society for the Turin Shroud Newsletter* 65 (June 2007): 10–27.

Frei, Max. "Nine Years of Palinological Studies on the Shroud." June 1982. Shroud of Turin website. https://shroud.com/pdfs/ssi-03part3.pdf.

Frequently Asked Questions, Shroud of Turin website. https://www.shroud.com/faq.htm#3.

Garlaschelli, Luigi. "Life-Size Reproduction of the Shroud of Turin and Its Image." *Journal of Imaging Science and Technology* 54 (July/

August 2010). https://library.imaging.org/jist/articles/54/4/art00002.

Goodacre, Mark. "'Finding Jesus': Shroud of Turin Q&A." CNN, February 9, 2017. https://www.cnn.com/2015/03/03/living/finding-jesus-q-a-shroud-turin/index.html.

Guscin, Mark. *The Image of Edessa*. Leiden: Brill, 2009.

———. "The Sudarium of Oviedo: Its History and Relationship to the Shroud of Turin." Shroud of Turin website, 1997. https://www.shroud.com/guscin.htm.

Hatch, Trevan G. *A Stranger in Jerusalem: Seeeing Jesus as a Jew*. Eugene, OR: Wipf & Stock, 2019.

Hengel, Martin. *Crucifixion*. Philadelphia: Fortress Press, 1977.

Horsley, Richard A., and Neil Asher Silberman. *The Message and the Kingdom: How Jesus and Paul Ignited a Revolution and Transformed the Ancient World*. Minneapolis: Fortress Press, 2002.

Jackson, John, Keith Propp, Rebecca Jackson, Ares Koumis, Jim Bertrand, and Bob Siefker. *The Shroud of Turin: A Critical Summary of Observations, Data and Hypotheses*. 2017. Turin Shroud Center of Colorado, https://www.shroudofturin.com/Resources/CRTSUM.pdf.

Jackson, John P., Eric J. Jumper, and William Ercoline. "Correlation of Image Intensity on the Turin Shroud Structure of Human Body Shape." *Applied Optics* 23 (1984): 2244–2270.

Jacoby, Douglas A. *Compelling Evidence for God and the Bible: Finding Truth in an Age of Doubt*. Eugene, OR: Harvest House Publishers.

The Jerome Biblical Commentary. Vols. 1 and 2. Edited by Raymond E. Brown, Joseph A. Fitzmyer, and Roland E. Murphy. Englewood Cliffs, NJ: Prentice-Hall Inc., 1968.

John Paul II. Address during a pastoral visit to Vercelli and Turin, May 24, 1998. https://www.vatican.va/content/john-paul-ii/en/travels/1998/documents/hf_jp-ii_spe_24051998_sindone.html.

———. Encyclical letter *Fides et Ratio* (September 14, 1998). Vatican website. https://www.vatican.va/content/john-paul-ii/en/encyclicals/documents/hf_jp-ii_enc_14091998_fides-et-ratio.html.

Johnson, Luke Timothy. *Jesus and the Gospels*. Chantilly, VA: The Great Courses, 2004.

———. *The Real Jesus: The Misguided Quest for the Historical Jesus and the Truth of the Traditional Gospels*. San Francisco: Harper San Francisco, 1977.

Jones, Roger. "Leonardo da Vinci: Anatomist." *British Journal of General Practice* 65, no. 599 (June 2012). National Library of Medicine. https://www.ncbi.nlm.nih.gov/pmc/articles/PMC3361109/.

Josephus, Flavius. *Antiquities of the Jews*. Translated by William Whiston. Auburn: John E. Beardsley, 1895. Perseus Digital Library. Tufts University. https://www.perseus.tufts.edu/hopper/text?doc=Perseus%3Atext%3A1999.01.0146%3Abook%3D4%3Asection%3D219.

———. *Jewish Antiquities*, Books XVIII–XX. Translated by Louis H. Feldman. Edited by T. E. Page, E Capps, W. H. D. Rouse, L. A. Post, and E. H. Warmington. Cambridge, MA: Harvard University Press, 1965.

———. *The Works of Flavius Josephus*. Translated by William Whiston. Revised by Rev. A. R. Shilleto. Vol. 2. London: George Bell and Sons, 1889.

Keener, Craig. S. *A Commentary on the Gospel of Matthew*. Grand Rapids, MI: Wm. B. Eerdmans, 1999.

———. *The Gospel of Matthew: A Socio-Rhetorical Commentary*. Grand Rapids, MI: Wm. B. Eerdmans, 2009.

Leitch, Peter Royston. "An Analysis of the Problems Involved in Our Contemporary Understanding of how the Man of the Shroud Was Nailed to the Cross." Shroud of Turin website. https://www.shroud.com/pdfs/n54part9.pdf.

Lewis, C. S., *Mere Christianity*. New York: Macmillan, 1952.

Little, Kitty. "The Formation of the Shroud's Body Image." Shroud of Turin website. https://www.shroud.com/pdfs/n46part7.pdf.

Long, Philip J. "James and Paul." Reading Acts, February 18, 2014. https://readingacts.com/2014/02/18/james-and-paul/.

Marinelli, Emanuela, and Marco Fasol. *Light from the Sepulchre*: Inquiry about the authenticity of the Shroud and the Gospel. Translated by Michela Marinelli. Fort Collins, CO: Gondolin Press, 2017.

McCrone, Walter C. *Judgment Day for the Shroud of Turin*. Amherst, NY: Prometheus Books, 1999.

Meier, John P. *A Marginal Jew: Rethinking the Historical Jesus*. Vol. 1, *The Roots of the Problem and the Person*. New Haven, CT: Yale University Press, 1991.

NAPA Institute. "The Latest Scientific Evidence of God and the Soul — Fr Robert Spitzer." YouTube video, 38:57. December 17, 2022. https://www.youtube.com/watch?v=KvghlgftwnE.

"New Evidence for the Shroud of Turin w/ Fr. Andrew Dalton." YouTube video, 3:07:39. Posted by Pints with Aquinas, January 6, 2023. https://www.youtube.com/watch?v=HAbuG-oVq1Q.

Nicolotti, Andrea. *From the Mandylion of Edessa to the Shroud of Turin: The Metamorphosis and Manipulation of a Legend*. Leiden: Brill, 2014.

———. "The Scourge of Jesus and the Roman Scourge: Historical and Archaeological Evidence." *Journal for the Study of the Historical Jesus* 15, no. 1 (2017): 1–59. https://doi.org/10.1163/17455197-01501006.

———. *The Shroud of Turin: The History and Legends of the World's Most Famous Relic*. Translated by Jeffrey M. Hunt and R. A. Smith. Waco, TX: Baylor University Press, 2019.

Orlando, Robert. *Apostle Paul: A Polite Bribe*. Eugene, OR: Cascade Books, 2014.

Parousia Media. "Parousia Podcast — Science, The Shroud of Turin and The Resurrection — Fr Robert J. Spitzer S.J. Ph.D. " YouTube video, 1:10:21. https://www.youtube.com/watch?v=au1bozyqcLs.

"Paul Vignon." Shroud of Turin website. https://www.shroud.com/pdfs/ssi06part7.pdf.

Price, Randall, with H. Wayne House. *Zondervan Handbook of Biblical Archaeology: A Book by Book Guide to Archaeological Discoveries Related to the Bible*. Grand Rapids, MI: Zondervan, 2017.

Price, Robert M. "Atheist Debates on the Historicity of Jesus." YouTube video, 41:07. Posted by Matt Dillahunty. https://www.youtube.com/watch?v=3NLXTGesqxA&t=1s.

———. "The Quest of the Mythical Jesus." The Jesus Project. Center for Inquiry. https://web.archive.org/web/20170417205223/http://www.centerforinquiry.net/jesusproject/articles/the_quest_of_the_mythical_jesus.

The Revised Standard Version of the Bible, Catholic Edition. Washington, D.C.: National Council of the Churches of Christ, 1966.

Robinson, John A. T. "Re-investigating the Shroud of Turin." *Theology* 80, no. 675 (1977): 193–197.

Ruffin, Bernard. *The Shroud of Turin: The Most Up-to-Date Analysis of All the Facts Regarding the Church's Controversial Relic*. Huntington, IN: Our Sunday Visitor, 1999.

Schwalbe, L. A., and R. N. Rogers. "Physics and Chemistry of the Shroud of Turin: A Summary of the 1978 Investigation." *Shroud of Turin Research Project* 135, no. 1 (1982): 3–49.

Schwortz, Barrie M. "Is the Shroud of Turin a Medieval Photograph?" Shroud of Turin website. https://www.shroud.com/pdfs/orvieto.pdf.

Shroud of Turin website. https://www.shroud.com.

Stevenson, Kenneth E., and Gary R. Habermas, *The Shroud and the Controversy: Science, Skepticism, and the Search for Authenticity.* Nashville: Thomas Nelson Publishers, 1990.

———. *Verdict on the Shroud: Evidence for the Death and Resurrection of Jesus Christ.* Ann Arbor, MI: Servant Books, 1980.

"A Summary of STURP's Conclusions." Shroud of Turin website. https://www.shroud.com/78conclu.htm.

Tadié, Solène. "Holy Shroud of Turin's Authenticity Can No Longer Be Disputed, Expert Asserts." *National Catholic Register,* December 30, 2022. https://www.ncregister.com/interview/holy-shroud-of-turin-s-authenticity-can-no-longer-be-disputed-expert-asserts.

"The 1978 STURP Team." Shroud of Turin website.https://www.shroud.com/78team.htm.

Thurston, Herbert. "The Holy Shroud and the Verdict of History." *Month* 101 (1903): 17–29.

———. "Shroud, The Holy." In *The Catholic Encyclopedia.* Vol. 13. Edited by Charles G. Herbermann et al. New York: Robert Appleton, 1912.

Turley, K. V. "A Holy Week Interview with a Shroud Researcher, Now a Catholic Convert." *National Catholic Register,* April 11, 2020. https://www.ncregister.com/news/a-holy-week-interview-with-a-shroud-researcher-now-a-catholic-convert.

Verschuuren, Gerard. *A Catholic Scientist Champions the Shroud of Turin.* Manchester, NH: Sophia Institute Press, 2021.

Vignon, Paul. *The Shroud of Christ.* Westminster: Archibald Constable, 1902.

Weisberger, Mindy. "Was the 'Nazareth Inscription" a Roman Response to Jesus' Empty Tomb? New Evidence Says It Wasn't," Live Science, April 17, 2020, https://www.livescience.com/nazareth-inscription-jesus-tomb-reinterpreted.html.

Whanger, Alan D. "Knowing a Hawk from a Handsaw." Shroud of Turin website. https://www.shroud.com/bsts4704.htm.

Wilson, Ian. *Murder at Golgotha: A Scientific Investigation into the Last Days of Jesus' Life, His Death, and His Resurrection*. New York: St. Martin's Griffin, 2006.

———. *The Shroud: Fresh Light on the 2000-Year-Old Mystery*. London: Bantam Press, 2010.

———. *The Shroud of Turin: Burial Cloth of Jesus?* Garden City, NY: Image Books, 1979.

Wilson, Ian, and Barrie Schwortz. *The Turin Shroud: The Illustrated Evidence*. London: Michael O'Mara, 2000.

Witherington, Ben III. *Acts of the Apostles: A Socio-Rhetorical Commentary*. Grand Rapids, MI: Eerdmans, 1998.

———. *The Jesus Quest: The Third Search for the Jew of Nazareth*. Downers Grove, IL: IVP Academic, 1997.

Wright, N. T. *The Resurrection of the Son of God: Christian Origins and the Question of God*. Vol. 3. Minneapolis: Fortress Press, 2003.

"Yves Delage." Shroud of Turin website. https://www.shroud.com/pdfs/ssi41part4.pdf.

Zugibe, Frederick T. *The Cross and the Shroud: A Medical Examiner Investigates the Crucifixion*. Smithtown, NY: Exposition Press, 1982.

———. *The Crucifixion of Jesus: A Forensic Inquiry*. New York: M. Evans and Company, 2005.

Endnotes

1 Matthew 27:33.

2 See Romans 1:18–21: "For the wrath of God is revealed from heaven against all ungodliness and wickedness of men who by their wickedness suppress the truth. For what can be known about God is plain to them, because God has shown it to them. Ever since the creation of the world his invisible nature, namely, his eternal power and deity, has been clearly perceived in the things that have been made. So they are without excuse; for although they knew God they did not honor him as God or give thanks to him, but they became futile in their thinking and their senseless minds were darkened."

See also Romans 2:13-16: "For it is not the hearers of the law who are righteous before God, but the doers of the law who will be justified. When Gentiles who have not the law do by nature what the law requires, they are a law to themselves, even though they do not have the law. They show that what the law requires is written on their hearts, while their conscience also bears witness and their conflicting thoughts accuse or perhaps excuse them on that day when, according to my gospel, God judges the secrets of men by Christ Jesus."

3 Dale C. Allison Jr., *The Resurrection of Jesus: Apologetics, Polemics, History* (London: Bloomsbury, 2021), 317.

4 John P. Meier, *A Marginal Jew: Rethinking the Historical Jesus,* vol. 1, *The Roots of the Problem and the Person* (New York: Doubleday, 1991), 8.

5 Luke 3:23.

6 Matthew 23:1–12: "Then said Jesus to the crowds and to his disciples, 'The scribes and the Pharisees sit on Moses' seat; so practice and observe whatever they tell you, but not what they do; for they preach, but do not practice. . . .' "

7 John 2:19.

8 Acts 10:37–38; Matthew 16:13–18; John 18:36–38.

9 N. T. Wright, *The Resurrection of the Son of God: Christian Origins and the Question of God*, vol. 3 (Minneapolis: Fortress Press, 2003), 140–141.

10 "Most of the crowd spread their garments on the road, and others cut branches from the trees and spread them on the road. And the crowds that went before him and that followed him shouted, 'Hosanna to the Son of David! Blessed is he who comes in the name of the Lord! Hosanna in the highest!' And when he entered Jerusalem, all the city was stirred, saying, 'Who is this?' And the crowds said, 'This is the prophet Jesus from Nazareth of Galilee'" (Matthew 21:8–11).

11 Matthew 21:1-11.

12 *Messiah*, or *mashiach* in Hebrew, meant "anointed one." The Jewish people believed prophesies in the Old Testament that God would send a deliverer to reestablish them as rulers of the Promised Land.

13 Ben Witherington III, *The Jesus Quest: The Third Search for the Jew of Nazareth* (Downers Grove, IL: IVP Academic, 1997), 16.

14 The Synoptic Gospels (Matthew, Mark, and Luke) date the Last Supper on the day of the Passover. John's Gospel, on the other hand, claims that this meal was held on the day of preparation for the Passover.

15 Ian Wilson, *Murder at Golgotha: A Scientific Investigation into the Last Days of Jesus' Life, His Death, and His Resurrection* (New York: St. Martin's Griffin, 2006), 37–38.

16 Some scholars note that *Iscariot* could be loosely translated to mean "dagger man," as he may have been an anti-Roman terrorist.

17 Matthew 26:14–16.

18 Matthew 26:36–56; Mark 14:32–50; Luke 22:39–53; John 18:1–12.

19 John 18:1.

20 Matthew 26:63–68.

21 John 18:28–32: "Then they led Jesus from the house of Caiaphas to the praetorium. It was early. They themselves did not enter the praetorium, so that they might not be defiled, but might eat the passover. So Pilate went out to them and said, 'What accusation do you bring against this man?' They answered him, 'If this man were not an evildoer, we would not have handed him over.' Pilate said to them, 'Take him yourselves and judge him by your own law.' The Jews said to him, 'It is not lawful for us to put any man to death.' This was to fulfil the word which Jesus had spoken to show by what death he was to die."

22 Jesus' cleansing of the Temple (Luke 19:45–48) is one of the most highly noted passages of Scripture. Some have used the verses to validate the destruction of property, while others have claimed that the passage gives merit to violence in specific situations. Perhaps it is easy to make these assumptions if one fails to consider the full context of the passage. In cleansing the Temple, particularly the Court of Gentiles, Jesus' purpose was to further the messianic mission that had been set before him by his Father.

23 Luke 23:1–5.

24 There are mixed views about how willing Pilate was to enforce punishment, though the biblical account makes him seem reluctant, and there is matching evidence in secular sources.

25 Mark 15:6–15.

26 Matthew 27:32; Mark 15:21; Luke 23:26.

27 Ian Wilson, *Murder at* Golgotha, 86–87.

28 "So where was Golgotha? In Hebrew the word *golgothe* means skull. This translates into Latin as hence the use of Calvary as an alternative name for the site. When Emperor Constantine's mother Helena made her visit to Jerusalem in A.D. 327, it was she who ordered the demolition of a temple of Venus built over the site, and who thereby found both Jesus' tomb and the Golgotha hillock on which he had been crucified. Both locations, being relatively close to each other, her son Constantine then enshrined both locations in a single, great Church of the Holy Sepulchre. Though this went through many destructions and rebuildings as Muslims and Crusaders later fought over the Holy Land, Jerusalem's present Church of the Holy Sepulchre undoubtedly occupies the sites that were first rediscovered by Empress Helena." Wilson, *Murder at Golgotha*, 90.

29 Raymond E. Brown, *A Crucified Christ in Holy Week* (Collegeville, MN: Liturgical Press, 1986), 43.

30 Martin Hengel, *Crucifixion* (Philadelphia: Fortress Press, 1977), 54.

31 Hengel, *Crucifixion*, 33–38.

32 Frederick Zugibe argues that he has disproven this theory of asphyxiation. See *The Cross and the Shroud: A Medical Examiner Investigates the Crucifixion* (Smithtown, NY: Exposition Press, 1982), 89–115.

33 Kenneth E. Stevenson and Gary R. Habermas, *The Shroud and the Controversy: Science, Skepticism, and the Search for Authenticity* (Nashville, TN: Thomas Nelson Publishers, 1990), 114.

34 Mark 15:42–47.

35 Dale C. Allison Jr., *The Resurrection of Jesus: Apologetics, Polemics, History* (London, UK: Bloomsbury Publishing, 2021), 97.

36 Matthew 27:57–61; Luke 23:50–53; John 19:38–41.

37 Wright, *The Resurrection of the Son of God*, 637.

38 Stevenson and Habermas, *The Shroud and the Controversy*, 114.

39 See Raymond E. Brown, *The Death of the Messiah: From Gethsemane to the Grave*, London: Geoffrey Chapman, 1994, pp. 1310-1313.

40 Many scholars dispute the historicity of the claim that guards were stationed at the tomb based on seeming contradictions in Scripture. For example, once they discover the empty tomb, Mary Magdalene and some of the disciples were reportedly afraid that Jesus' body had been stolen. It seems that they were not aware that Jesus would rise. So how did the Jewish authorities anticipate that the disciples would try to steal the body to make it look like a resurrection, if the disciples didn't even know themselves? See Dale C. Allison, *Resurrecting Jesus: The Earliest Christian Tradition and Its Interpreters* (New York: T&T Clark International, 2005), 311. See also *The Jerome Biblical Commentary*, vols. 1 and 2, ed. Raymond E. Brown, Joseph A. Fitzmyer, and Roland E. Murphy (Englewood Cliffs, NJ: Prentice-Hall, 1968), 794; Peter Annet, *The Resurrection of Jesus in Answer to the Tryal of the Witnesses* (London: M. Cooper, 1744). See also Amos N. Wilder's argument for the inherent truth in the Bible in Craig A. Evans, ed., *The Historical Jesus: Critical Concepts in Religious Studies*, vol. 1 (London: Routledge, 2004), 367.

41 Matthew 27:62–66.

42 Deuteronomy 19:15.

43 Brown, *Death of the Messiah*, 1294–1296.

44 Craig A. Evans and Tom Wright, *Jesus: The Final Days*, ed. Troy A. Miller (London: Society for Promoting Christian Knowledge, 2008), 70.

45 Matthew 28:1; Mark 16:1; Luke 24:1; John 20:1.

46 Robert M. Price, "Atheist Debates on the Historicity of Jesus," YouTube video, 41:07, posted by Matt Dillahunty, https://www.youtube.com/watch?v=3NLXTGesqxA&t=1s.

47 Bart D. Ehrman, "Did Jesus Exist?," *Huffington Post*, May 20, 2012, https://www.huffpost.com/entry/did-jesus-exist_b_1349544.

48 Robert M. Price, "The Quest of the Mythical Jesus," The Jesus Project, Center for Inquiry, https://web.archive.org/web/20170417205223/http://www.centerforinquiry.net/jesusproject/articles/the_quest_of_the_mythical_jesus.

49 *The Historical Jesus, Jesus at the Vanishing Point* (argued by Robert M. Price) (Downers Grove, IL: InterVarsity Press, 2009), 75.

50 Douglas A. Jacoby, *Compelling Evidence for God and the Bible: Finding Truth in an Age of Doubt* (Eugene, OR: Harvest House Publishers), 97.

51 Bart Ehrman, *Peter, Paul, and Mary Magdalene: The Followers of Jesus in History and Legend* (New York: Oxford University Press, 2006), 26.

52 Ibid.

53 Meier, *A Marginal Jew*, 89–90.

54 Hengel, *Crucifixion*, 2–3.

55 See Meier, *A Marginal Jew*, 56–89, for more on the historical Jesus as described by Josephus.

56 Luke Timothy Johnson, *The Real Jesus: The Misguided Quest for the Historical Jesus and the Truth of the Traditional Gospels* (San Francisco: Harper San Francisco, 1977), 114.

57 Gerard Verschuuren, *A Catholic Scientist Champions the Shroud of Turin* (Manchester, NH: Sophia Institute Press), 15–16.

58 Ehrman, "Did Jesus Exist?"

59 Bart D. Ehrman, *Did Jesus Exist? The Historical Argument for Jesus of Nazareth* (New York: Harper One, 2012), 38–39.

60 Bart D. Ehrman, "Are the Gospels Historically Reliable? The Problem of Contradictions," YouTube video, 59:18, June 27, 2020, https://www.youtube.com/watch?v=AymnA526j9U.

61 Ehrman, "Did Jesus Exist?"

62 David L. Allen, *Lukan Authorship of Hebrews* (Nashville, TN: B&H Publishing Group, 2010).

63 Richard A. Horsley and Neil Asher Silberman, *The Message and the Kingdom: How Jesus and Paul Ignited a Revolution and Transformed the Ancient World* (Minneapolis: Fortress Press, 2002), 147–148.

64 Craig A. Evans, *Jesus and His World: The Archaeological Evidence* (Louisville, KY: Westminster John Knox Press, 2012), 6.

65 Several books in the Bible recount the interactions and relationship of James and Paul in the early years of the church. See Acts 15, Acts 21, Galatians 1, Galatians 2, and Romans 15. In the Apocryphal Writings of the Pseudo- Clementines, they are in direct aggressive conflict. Philip J. Long, "James and Paul," Reading Acts, February 18, 2014, https://readingacts.com/2014/02/18/james-and-paul/.

66 D. C. Allison and W. D. Davies, *Matthew 8–18, International Critical Commentary*, vol. 2 (London: T&T Clark International, 2006), 458.

67 Ehrman, "Did Jesus Exist?"

68 Ben Witherington III, *Acts of the Apostles: A Socio-Rhetorical Commentary* (Grand Rapids, MI: Eerdmans, 1998), 32.

69 Bart Ehrman, "The Greek Manuscripts of the New Testament," *The Bart Ehrman Blog*, October 29, 2022, https://ehrmanblog.org/

the-greek-manuscripts-of-the-new-testament/?utm_source=rss&utm_medium=rss&utm_campaign=the-greek-manuscripts-of-the-new-testament.

70 Ehrman, *Peter, Paul, and Mary Magdalene*, 183.

71 Wilson, *Murder at Golgotha*, 119. Also see *Encyclopaedia Romana*, s.v. "The Death of Jesus," https://penelope.uchicago.edu/~grout/encyclopaedia_romana/calendar/jesus.html.

72 Mark 16:9.

73 Mark 16:1.

74 Luke 23:54–56; 24:1–3.

75 Flavius Josephus, *Antiquities of the Jews*, trans. William Whiston (Auburn: John E. Beardsley, 1895), 4:219, Perseus Digital Library, Tufts University, https://www.perseus.tufts.edu/hopper/text?doc=Perseus%3Atext%3A1999.01.0146%3Abook%3D4%3Asection%3D219.

76 Allison, *The Resurrection of Jesus*, 112.

77 Randall Price with H. Wayne House, *Zondervan Handbook of Biblical Archaeology: A Book by Book Guide to Archaeological Discoveries Related to the Bible* (Grand Rapids, MI: Zondervan, 2017), 259.

78 Trevan G. Hatch, *A Stranger in Jerusalem: Seeing Jesus as a Jew* (Eugene, OR: Wipf & Stock, 2019), 35.

79 Craig S. Keener, *The Gospel of Matthew: A Socio-Rhetorical Commentary* (Grand Rapids, MI: Wm. B. Eerdmans2009), 714.

80 Raymond E. Brown, *An Introduction to the New Testament* (New York: Doubleday, 1997), 202–203.

81 John 20:1–2.

82 Mark 16:11.

83 John 20:3–10.

84 Matthew 28:11–15.

85 John 20:3–7.

86 Ian Wilson, *The Shroud: Fresh Light on the 2000-Year-Old Mystery* (London: Bantam Press, 2010), 82.

87 Kenneth E. Stevenson and Gary R. Habermas, *Verdict on the Shroud: Evidence for the Death and Resurrection of Jesus Christ* (Ann Arbor, MI: Servant Books, 1980), 42.

88 Ibid.

89 John 20:6–8.

90 John 11:44: "The dead man [Lazarus] came out, his hands and feet bound with bandages, and his face wrapped with a cloth."

91 Luke 24:12.

92 Luke 24:36–37.

93 See *The Works of Flavius Josephus*, trans. William Whiston, rev. by Rev. A. R. Shilleto, vol. 2 (London: George Bell and Sons, 1889).

94 Some have speculated that, early on, the Shroud was folded up and hidden in a clay jar. Examinations of the Shroud have shown that there are water stains on the cloth. Water could have pooled at the bottom of the jar and damaged the linen. The stains are also symmetrical, suggesting that the Shroud was folded when it was exposed to the water. Paul might hint at this in 2 Corinthians 4:7: "But we have this treasure in earthen vessels, to show that the transcendent power belongs to God and not to us." Paul may have also meant this passage figuratively, according to his style. We are the "earthen vessels" in which the Holy Spirit lives. See J. Christiaan Beker, *Paul the Apostle: The Triumph of God in Life and Thought* (Philadelphia: Fortress Press, 1980).

95 Stevenson and Habermas, *The Shroud and the Controversy*, 73–74.

96 Wilson, *The Shroud*, 178–179.

97 Andrea Nicolotti, *The Shroud of Turin: The History and Legends of the World's Most Famous Relic*, trans. Jeffrey M. Hunt and R. A. Smith (Waco, TX: Baylor University Press, 2019), 299–303.

98 Rev. Paul De Gail, S.J., "Paul Vignon," Shroud of Turin website, https://www.shroud.com/pdfs/ssi06part7.pdf.

99 Solène Tadié, "Holy Shroud of Turin's Authenticity Can No Longer Be Disputed, Expert Asserts," *National Catholic Register*, December 20, 2022, https://www.ncregister.com/interview/holy-shroud-of-turin-s-authenticity-can-no-longer-be-disputed-expert-asserts.

100 Stevenson and Habermas, *Verdict on the Shroud*, 16.

101 Nicolotti argues that the Image of Edessa, or Mandylion, is indeed a fraud in *The Shroud of Turin*, 393–398.

102 Ian Wilson, *The Shroud of Turin: Burial Cloth of Jesus?* (Garden City, NY: Image Books, 1979), 112–124.

103 Verschuuren, *A Catholic Scientist*, 39–40.

104 Wilson, *The Shroud*, 20.

105 Verschuuren, *A Catholic Scientist*, 39. See Ian Wilson's argument supporting the theory that this was the Shroud of Turin in *The Shroud*, 178–196.

106 Nicolotti, *The Shroud of Turin*, 393.

107 Parousia Media, "Parousia Podcast — Science, The Shroud of Turin and The Resurrection — Fr Robert J. Spitzer S.J. Ph.D, " YouTube video, 1:10:21, https://www.youtube.com/watch?v=au1bozyqcLs.

108 For more information on the Sudarium, see Mark Guscin, "The Sudarium of Oviedo: Its History and Relationship to the Shroud of Turin," Shroud of Turin website, 1997, https://www.shroud.com/guscin.htm.

109 Guscin, "The Sudarium of Oviedo."

110 Wilson, *The Shroud*, 178–196.

111 Verschuuren, *A Catholic Scientist*, 40.

112 Ibid., 38.

113 Stevenson and Habermas, *The Shroud and the Controversy*, 55.

114 Nicolotti records de Clari's passage in *The Shroud of Turin*, 43–44.

115 Jack Markwardt suggests that the Cathars in Languedoc, France, may have been in possession of the Shroud during this gap in the historical record. See "Was the Shroud in Languedoc during the Missing Years?," 1997, Shroud of Turin website, https://www.shroud.com/markward.htm.

116 Verschuuren, *A Catholic Scientist*, 37.

117 Stevenson and Habermas, *Verdict on the Shroud*, 18–21.

118 Wilson, *The Shroud*, 277.

119 Verschuuren, *A Catholic Scientist*, 35.

120 Wilson, *The Shroud*, 145.

121 Verschuuren, *A Catholic Scientist*, 35.

122 Wilson, *The Shroud*, 9.

123 Verschuuren, *A Catholic Scientist*, 34–35. The nuns at the chapel describe how the fire nearly destroyed the prized relic. Dorothy Crispino, "The Report of the Poor Clare Nuns: Chambéry, 1534," Shroud of Turin website, https://www.shroud.com/pdfs/ssi02part6.pdf.

124 See Nicolotti, *The Shroud of Turin*, 256–257.

125 Sindonology is the formal study of the Shroud of Turin.

126 See Nicolotti, *The Shroud of Turin*, 253.

127 Giuseppe Enrie recalls how Pia reacted to his discovery: "He [Pia] devoted himself to a more attentive observation; and, there, in a few moments, as he sensed something extraordinary, an image formed and was there on the plate, unmistakable; but instead of a negative image, it was the positive shape and characteristics of a man, with a face clear as if it were a portrait, amazing, never seen, magnificent, the true face of Christ. That same photographer and those who assisted him recounted that he nearly fell ill, and his hands, trembling and awkward in the difficult manipulation of the large glass plate, which became slippery through contact with the bath, did not allow it to fall or strike harmfully against any object while maneuvering it to the soft, reddish glow of the laboratory. Only by great self-control did Pia succeed in bringing the

process of developing the image to an end and place the plate in the fix bath to relinquish it safely." Nicolotti, *The Shroud of Turin*, 257–258.

128 EWTN, "The Mystery of the Shroud of Turin," *EWTN News Nightly*, October 11, 2021, 2023, https://www.youtube.com/watch?v=MTmO_9Xy0E0.

129 Wilson, *The Shroud*, 44.

130 Ibid., 43–44, "As Enrie would later recall of the natural-size negative plate of the Shroud man's face (pl. 5), 'I will remember as one of the most beautiful moments of my life, certainly the most moving of my career, the instant in which I submitted my perfect plate to the avid look of the Archbishop and that select whole group of people.' Among that 'select whole group of people' crowding around the plate was the crown prince Umberto in whose honour the Shroud had been displayed. According to Enrie's description, 'The young prince was almost beside himself with excitement and emotion.'

"That same glass plate, which I personally studied at Enrie's old studio in 1994, is now a historic object in its own right. Today it can be viewed in Turin's Museum of the Shroud. It speaks for itself. In the light of that glass plate, and the literally thousands of similar negative photographs of the Shroud face, both professional and amateur, that have since followed it, any suggestion that the phenomenon Pia first brought to light back in 1898 was some kind of hoax could now be dismissed out of hand. And, thankfully, Pia, although now seventy-six, was still alive to see his work thus vindicated. He had been invited to be present at the showing, along with a public notary and photographic experts to make absolutely sure that Enrie, in his turn, could not be accused of any trickery."

131 "Yves Delage," Shroud of Turin website, https://www.shroud.com/pdfs/ssi41part4.pdf.

132 Ibid.

133 Wilson, *The Shroud*, 44.

134 Verschuuren, *A Catholic Scientist*, 64.

135 Ibid., 64–65.

136 Wilson, *The Shroud*, 194.

137 Paul Vignon, *The Shroud of Christ* (Westminster: Archibald Constable, 1902).

138 Alan D. Whanger, "Knowing a Hawk from a Handsaw," Shroud of Turin website, https://www.shroud.com/bsts4704.htm.

139 Barrie Schwortz, photographer on the Shroud of Turin Research Project team, answers questions about the discovery of the coins on the Shroud image. Frequently Asked Questions, Shroud of Turin website, https://www.shroud.com/faq.htm#3.

140 Ibid.

141 Maggie Ciskanik, "5 Key Pieces of Evidence on the Shroud of Turin," Magis Center, August 7, 2018, https://www.magiscenter.com/blog/5-key-pieces-of-evidence-on-the-shroud-of-turin.

142 Nicolotti questions the veracity of Frei's findings and records the various legitimate objections to his pollen studies in *The Shroud of Turin*, 346–349 and 367–370. Also see Walter C. McCrone, *Judgment Day for the Shroud of Turin* (Amherst, NY: Prometheus Books, 1999), 27–30.

143 Nicolotti, *The Shroud of Turin*, 368.

144 Avinoam Danin, "Pressed Flowers: Where Did the Shroud of Turin Originate? A Botanical Quest," *Eretz* (November–December 1997), Shroud of Turin website, https://www.shroud.com/danin.htm.

145 Others claim that the only precedent of this type of weave, a herringbone weave, can be seen only as early as the Middle Ages. See Allison, *The Resurrection of Jesus*, 319.

146 Roger Jones, "Leonardo da Vinci: Anatomist," *British Journal of General Practice* 62, no. 599 (June 2012), National Library of Medicine, https://www.ncbi.nlm.nih.gov/pmc/articles/PMC3361109/.

147 Emanuela Marinelli and Marco Fasol, *Light from the Sepulchre*: Inquiry about the authenticity of the Shroud and the Gospel, trans. Michela Marinelli (Fort Collins, CO: Gondolin Press, 2017), 46–50.

148 Ibid., 44–45.

149 Stevenson and Habermas, *Verdict on the Shroud*, 73–74.

150 Wilson, *The Shroud*, 111–112.

151 Marinelli and Fasol, *Light from the Sepulchre*, 58.

152 Meier, *A Marginal Jew*, 387–388.

153 Marinelli and Fasol, *Light from the Sepulchre*, 58.

154 Stevenson and Habermas, *The Shroud and the Controversy*, 132–133.

155 Marinelli and Fasol, *Light from the Sepulchre*, 49.

156 Stevenson and Habermas, *The Shroud and the Controversy*, 130.

157 "Researcher Questions Whether Shroud Was Present at Last Supper," Catholic News Agency, April 27, 2006, https://www.catholicnewsagency.com/news/6595/researcher-questions-whether-shroud-was-present-at-last-supper.

158 M. Antonacci, "Particle Radiation from the Body Could Explain the Shroud's Images and Its Carbon Dating," *Scientific Research and Essays* 7, no. 29 (July 12, 2012): 2622, Academic Journals, https://academicjournals.org/article/article1380798649_Antonacci.pdf.

159 Marinelli and Fasol, *Light from the Sepulchre*, 62.

160 Ibid., 63.

161 Parousia Media, "Parousia Podcast."

162 See Stevenson and Habermas, *The Shroud and the Controversy*, 139. "Some people might prefer to wait for a yet unknown or future naturalistic hypothesis. And, to be honest, there is some warrant for such attitudes in light of the recent carbon dating, for this is a serious objection. On the other hand, no known alternative thesis can presently explain the image."

163 See the description of this analysis on the Shroud of Turin website: https://www.shroud.com/78strp10.htm.

164 For more information on the VP-8 experiments, see https://www.shroud.com/78strp10.htm.

165 Wilson, *The Shroud*, 45.

166 Frederick T. Zugibe, *The Crucifixion of Jesus: A Forensic Inquiry* (New York: M. Evans and Company, 2005), 230.

167 Wilson, *The Shroud*, 44–46.

168 Ibid., 46.

169 "The 1978 STURP Team," Shroud of Turin website, https://www.shroud.com/78team.htm.

170 Bernard Ruffin, *The Shroud of Turin: The Most Up-to-Date Analysis of All the Facts Regarding the Church's Controversial Relic* (Huntington, IN: Our Sunday Visitor, 1999), 82–83.

171 Wilson, *The Shroud*, 90.

172 Ibid., 94.

173 "A Summary of STURP's Conclusions," Shroud of Turin website, https://www.shroud.com/78conclu.htm.

174 Ibid.

175 Nicolotti, *The Shroud of Turin*, 423.

176 Other renowned scholars, such as Mark Goodacre, disagree with the claim that the scientists' tests were innacurate. Mark Goodacre, "'Finding Jesus': Shroud of Turin Q&A," CNN, February 9, 2017, https://www.cnn.com/2015/03/03/living/finding-jesus-q-a-shroud-turin/index.html.

177 Pints With Aquinas, "New Evidence for the Shroud of Turin w/ Fr. Andrew Dalton," YouTube video, 3:07:39, posted by Pints with Aquinas, January 6, 2023, https://www.youtube.com/watch?v=HAbuG-oVq1Q.

178 Ibid.

179 Mark Antonacci, *Resurrection of the Shroud: New Scientific, Medical, and Archaeological Evidence* (New York: M. Evans, 2000), 179.

180 Associated Press, "Turin Shroud, '3,000 Years Old,'" *Guardian*, January 29, 2005, https://www.theguardian.com/world/2005/jan/29/religion.uk.

181 Parousia Media, "Parousia Podcast."

182 K. V. Turley, "A Holy Week Interview with a Shroud Researcher, Now a Catholic Convert," *National Catholic Register*, April 11, 2020, https://www.ncregister.com/news/a-holy-week-interview-with-a-shroud-researcher-now-a-catholic-convert.

183 T. Casabianca, E. Marinelli, G. Pernagallo, and B. Torrisi, "Radiocarbon Dating of the Turin Shroud: New Evidence from Raw Data," *Archaeometry* 61, no. 5 (March 22, 2019), https://philarchive.org/archive/CASTRD-3.

184 John Burger, New Data Questions Finding That Shroud of Turin Was a Medieval Hoax," Aleteia, July 22, 2019, https://aleteia.org/2019/07/22/new-data-questions-finding-that-shroud-of-turin-was-medieval-hoax/.

185 Parousia Media, "Parousia Podcast."

186 For more information on where missing edges of the Shroud of Turin might have ended up, see César Barta, "The Shroud Sent to Louis IX of France by Baldwin II, the Latin Emperor at Constantople," Shroud of Turin website, https://www.shroud.com/pdfs/n56part5.pdf.

187 Parousia Media, "Parousia Podcast." See also critiques of the invisible mending theory: Flury-Lemberg, Mechthild. "The Invisible Mending of Shroud in Theory and Reality." *British Society for the Turin Shroud Newsletter* 65 (June 2007): 10–27.

188 Martin M. Barillas, "Scientists Debunk Theory That Shroud of Turin Is Medieval Hoax," LifeSiteNews, July 24, 2019, https://www.lifesitenews.com/news/scientists-debunk-theory-that-shroud-of-turin-is-medieval-hoax/.

189 "New Evidence for the Shroud."

190 Casabianca, Marinelli, Pernagallo, Torrisi, "Radiocarbon Dating of the Turin Shroud."

191 John Paul II, address during a pastoral visit to Vercelli and Turin, May 24, 1998, https://www.vatican.va/content/john-paul-ii/en/travels/1998/documents/hf_jp-ii_spe_24051998_sindone.html.

192 Marinelli and Fasol, *Light from the Sepulchre*, 26–39.

193 Kitty Little, "The Formation of the Shroud's Body Image," Shroud of Turin website, https://www.shroud.com/pdfs/n46part7.pdf.

194 NAPA Institute, "The Latest Scientific Evidence of God and the Soul — Fr Robert Spitzer," YouTube video, 38:57, December 17, 2022, https://www.youtube.com/watch?v=KvghlgftwnE.

195 Stevenson and Habermas, *The Shroud and the Controversy*, 137.

196 Johnson, *The Real Jesus*, 110–111.

197 Ibid.

198 Verschuuren, *A Catholic Scientist*, 64.

199 Matthew 27:30; Mark 15:19; Luke 22:63–64; John 19:3.

200 Verschuuren, *A Catholic Scientist*, 22.

201 Wilson, *Murder at Golgotha*, 70–73.

202 Matthew 27:29; Mark 15:16–20; John 19:2–5.

203 Zugibe, *The Cross and the Shroud*, 33–35.

204 Ibid., 156–157.

205 Ibid., 150–151.

206 Wilson, *Murder at Golgotha*, 102–106.

207 Wilson, *The Shroud*, 65–67.

208 Verschuuren, *A Catholic Scientist*, 66–67.

209 Zugibe, *The Cross and the Shroud*, 160.

210 Ibid., 162–163.

211 Wilson, *Murder at Golgotha*, 114.

212 John 19:34.

213 John 8:12.

214 "Do not think that I have come to bring peace on earth; I have not come to bring peace, but a sword" (Matthew 10:34).

215 Matthew 23:1–4, 11–12.

216 Some say that Jesus' insistence on turning the other cheek can be seen as a form of resistance by showing indifference toward others' opinions of you. Craig S. Keener, *A Commentary on the Gospel of Matthew*, 197–198.

217 Matthew 21:12–13.

218 Matthew 21:12.

219 Matthew 26:64–65. See also N. T. Wright's thesis that Caiaphas was reacting to Jesus' confessing to sharing God's throne. *The Resurrection of the Son of God*, 643.

220 Matthew 2:1–4.

221 See N. T. Wright's discussion of Jesus' redefining of God's Kingdom in *The Resurrection of the Son of God*, 470–472, 644.

222 John 19:21–22. See also Luke Timothy Johnson, *Jesus and the Gospels* (Chantilly, VA: The Great Courses, 2004), 309–310.

223 See the diagram of the Shroud on page 130c in Stevenson and Habermas's *The Shroud and the Controversy* and the discussion of possible shoulder wounds that Christ endured in Peter Royston Leitch, "An Analysis of the Problems Involved in Our Contemporary Understanding of how the Man of

the Shroud Was Nailed to the Cross," Shroud of Turin website, https://www.shroud.com/pdfs/n54part9.pdf.

224 John 19:31–35.

225 Matthew 27:57–60.

226 Mark 15:44–47.

227 Mindy Weisberger, "Was the 'Nazareth Inscription' a Roman Response to Jesus' Empty Tomb? New Evidence Says It Wasn't," Live Science, April 17, 2020, https://www.livescience.com/nazareth-inscription-jesus-tomb-reinterpreted.html.

228 Evans and Wright, *Jesus: The Final Days*, 70.

229 John 20:1–9.

230 John 20:19–23.

231 See N. T. Wright's explication of the *soma pneumatikon* in *The Resurrection of the Son of God*, 354.

232 James D. G. Dunn, *The Cambridge Companion to St. Paul* (Cambridge, UK: Cambridge University Press, 2004), 168–169.

233 John 20:11–18.

234 John 20:25–29.

235 Matthew 19:16–22.

236 "Shroud of Turin Retreat — Fr. Andrew Dalton, LC, Talk 1," YouTube video, 56:59, posted by Real Faith Talks, March 26, 2019, https://www.youtube.com/watch?v=XcaPY2LsfKQ.

237 See Thomas Aquinas, *Compendium of Theology*, translated by Cyril Vollert (St. Louis, MO: B. Herder, 1947), 326. "To some extent God makes himself known to men through a certain natural knowledge, by imbuing them with the light of reason and by giving existence to visible creatures, in which are reflected some glimmerings of his goodness and wisdom, as we read in Romans 1:19: That which is known of God, that is, what is knowable about God by natural reason, is plain to them, namely, is disclosed to pagan peoples. Because God has shown it to them through the light of reason and through the creatures he has put in the world."

238 John 18:36. At Jesus' arrest, "when those who were about him saw what would follow, they said, 'Lord, shall we strike with the sword?' And one of them struck the slave of the high priest and cut off his right ear. But Jesus said, 'No more of this!' And he touched his ear and healed him" (Luke 22:49–51). Jesus was saying that that was not his way. His goal was the humble acceptance of his Father's will.

239 If faith and reason are intertwined as two sources of truth, then true wisdom comes only from following God's laws of nature and those laws he has revealed in divine revelation. Romans 1:24, 26, 28.

240 Matthew 16:24–25.

241 John A. T. Robinson, "Re-Investigating the Shroud of Turin," *Theology* 80, no. 675 (1977): 196.

242 See Luke 23:34.

243 Ian Wilson's *The Shroud* helped with this timeline.

244 Luke 23:6–12.

245 See Josephus, *Jewish Antiquities*, 496–497; see also Mustafa Akyol, *The Islamic Jesus: How the King of the Jews Became a Prophet of the Muslims* (New York: St. Martin's Press, 2017).

246 John 7:45–51.

247 Stephen Danto-Collins, *Legions of Rome: The Definitive History of Every Imperial Roman Legion* (New York: St. Martin's Press, 2010), 40.

About the Author

Robert Orlando, B.F.A., School of Visual Arts, is an award-winning author, filmmaker, and entrepreneur who founded Nexus Media. His studies include film, religion, ancient and modern history, and biography. As an award-winning writer and director, he has released more than a dozen movies, including the thought-provoking documentaries *Silence Patton, The Divine Plan,* and *Trump's Rosebud.* His books include *Apostle Paul: A Polite Bribe, The Divine Plan*, *The Tragedy of Patton*, *Citizen Trump: A One Man Show*, and *Apostle Paul: The Final Days* (2024). He published his script *The Road* in the book *Writing Short Scripts and has written several other screenplays.* His articles have appeared in the *American Thinker, The Catholic Thing, the Daily Caller, HuffPost, Patheos, and Merion West, and he has appeared on CBN, The Eric Metaxas Show, The Mike Huckabee Show, TNT, EWTN, and Newsmax. The Shroud* is Orlando's seventh book, with a film to follow. He resides in Princeton, New Jersey, where he is completing his graduate studies at Princeton Theological Seminary.

Sophia Institute

Sophia Institute is a nonprofit institution that seeks to nurture the spiritual, moral, and cultural life of souls and to spread the gospel of Christ in conformity with the authentic teachings of the Roman Catholic Church.

Sophia Institute Press fulfills this mission by offering translations, reprints, and new publications that afford readers a rich source of the enduring wisdom of mankind.

Sophia Institute also operates the popular online resource CatholicExchange.com. *Catholic Exchange* provides world news from a Catholic perspective as well as daily devotionals and articles that will help readers to grow in holiness and live a life consistent with the teachings of the Church.

In 2013, Sophia Institute launched Sophia Institute for Teachers to renew and rebuild Catholic culture through service to Catholic education. With the goal of nurturing the spiritual, moral, and cultural life of souls, and an abiding respect for the role and work of teachers, we strive to provide materials and programs that are at once enlightening to the mind and ennobling to the heart; faithful and complete, as well as useful and practical.

Sophia Institute gratefully recognizes the Solidarity Association for preserving and encouraging the growth of our apostolate over the course of many years. Without their generous and timely support, this book would not be in your hands.

www.SophiaInstitute.com
www.CatholicExchange.com
www.SophiaInstituteforTeachers.org